P9-CQO-920

JESUS AND YAHWEH

ALSO BY HAROLD BLOOM

Where Shall Wisdom Be Found? (2004)

The Best Poems of the English Language (2004)

Hamlet: Poem Unlimited (2003)

Genius: A Mosaic of One Hundred Exemplary Creative Minds (2002)

Stories and Poems for Extremely Intelligent Children of All Ages (2001)

How to Read and Why (2000)

Shakespeare: The Invention of the Human (1998)

Omens of Millennium (1996)

The Western Canon (1994)

The American Religion (1992)

The Book of J (1990)

Ruin the Sacred Truths (1989)

Poetics of Influence (1988)

The Strong Light of the Canonical (1987)

Agon: Towards a Theory of Revisionism (1982)

The Breaking of the Vessels (1982)

The Flight to Lucifer: A Gnostic Fantasy (1979)

Wallace Stevens: The Poems of Our Climate (1977)

Figures of Capable Imagination (1976)

Poetry and Repression (1976)

Kabbalah and Criticism (1975)

A Map of Misreading (1975)

The Anxiety of Influence (1973)

The Ringers in the Tower: Studies in Romantic Tradition (1971)

Yeats (1970)

Commentary on David V. Erdman's Edition of
The Poetry and Prose of William Blake (1965)

Blake's Apocalypse (1963)

The Visionary Company (1961)

Shelley's Mythmaking (1959)

JESUS *and* YAHWEH

THE NAMES DIVINE

HAROLD BLOOM

RIVERHEAD BOOKS

a member of Penguin Group (USA) Inc.

New York

2005

RIVERHEAD BOOKS
Published by the Penguin Group
Penguin Group (USA) Inc., 375 Hudson Street, New York, New York 10014, USA •
Penguin Group (Canada), 90 Eglinton Avenue East, Suite 700, Toronto, Ontario M4P 2Y3,
Canada (a division of Pearson Penguin Canada Inc.) • Penguin Books Ltd, 80 Strand,
London WC2R 0RL, England • Penguin Ireland, 25 St Stephen's Green, Dublin 2, Ireland
(a division of Penguin Books Ltd) • Penguin Group (Australia), 250 Camberwell Road,
Camberwell, Victoria 3124, Australia (a division of Pearson Australia Group Pty Ltd) •
Penguin Books India Pvt Ltd, 11 Community Centre, Panchsheel Park, New
Delhi–110 017, India • Penguin Group (NZ), Cnr Airborne and
Rosedale Roads, Albany, Auckland 1310, New Zealand (a division of Pearson
New Zealand Ltd) • Penguin Books (South Africa) (Pty) Ltd, 24 Sturdee Avenue,
Rosebank, Johannesburg 2196, South Africa

Penguin Books Ltd, Registered Offices:
80 Strand, London WC2R 0RL, England

Copyright © 2005 by Harold Bloom
All rights reserved. No part of this book may be reproduced, scanned, or distributed
in any printed or electronic form without permission. Please do not participate
in or encourage piracy of copyrighted materials in violation of the
author's rights. Purchase only authorized editions.
Published simultaneously in Canada

Library of Congress Cataloging-in-Publication Data

Bloom, Harold.
Jesus and Yahweh : the names divine / Harold Bloom.
p. cm.
ISBN 1-57322-322-0
1. Jesus Christ—History of doctrines.   2. God (Judaism)—History of doctrines.
3. Christianity and other religions—Judaism.   4. Judaism—Relations—Christianity.
I. Title.
BT198.B555   2005   2005046409
232.9'06—dc22

Printed in the United States of America
1   3   5   7   9   10   8   6   4   2

This book is printed on acid-free paper. ♾

Book design by Marysarah Quinn

FOR DONALD HARMAN AKENSON

ACKNOWLEDGMENTS

I am grateful to my editor, Celina Spiegel. I would also like to thank my research assistants, Brad Woodworth and Brett Foster, as well as my copy editor, Toni Rachiele, and my agents, Glen Hartley and Lynn Chu, and their associate Katy Sprinkel.

CONTENTS

PART II. YAHWEH

Tho thou art Worshipd by the Names Divine

Of Jesus & Jehovah, thou art still

The Son of Morn in weary Nights decline

The lost Travellers Dream under the Hill

—WILLIAM BLAKE, "The Gates of Paradise"

JESUS AND YAHWEH

INTRODUCTION

THIS BOOK centers upon three figures: a more-or-less historical person, Yeshua of Nazareth; a theological God, Jesus Christ; and a human, all-too-human God, Yahweh. That opening sentence cannot avoid sounding polemical, and yet I hope only to clarify (if I can) and not to give offense.

Almost everything that can be known about Yeshua emanates from the New Testament, and from allied or heretical writings. All these are tendentious: their designs upon us, as readers or auditors, are palpable and conversionary. If I call Yeshua "more-or-less historical," I mean only that nearly everything truly important about him reaches me from texts I cannot trust. Quests for "the historical Jesus" invariably fail, even those by the most responsible searchers. Questers, however careful, find themselves, and not the elusive and evasive Yeshua, enigma-of-enigmas. Every Christian believer I know, here or abroad, has her or his own Jesus. St. Paul admitted that he himself had become all things to all men: that may be the single authentic affinity the great Apostle had with his savior.

Though the historical Yeshua, however many yearn for him, never will be available to them, Jesus Christ is a theological God presented by rival traditions: Eastern Orthodoxy, Roman Catholicism, normative Protestantisms—Lutheranism, Calvinism, and their variants—and sects old and new, many of them American originals. Most of these myriad Christendoms would reject instantly my conclusion that Jesus Christ and his putative father, Yahweh, do not seem to be two persons of one substance, but of very different substances indeed. Yahweh, from Philo of Alexandria to the present, has been allegorized endlessly, but he is sublimely stubborn, and cannot be divested of his human, all-too-human traits of personality and of character. Since he appears to have chosen exile or eclipse, here and now, or perhaps is guilty of desertion, one sees why theological Gods have displaced him. Jesus Christ, the Holy Spirit, and the Virgin Mother Mary have become the pragmatic Trinity. Yahweh either dwindles into a remote God the Father, or blends into the identity of Jesus Christ. I am merely descriptive, and hope to disengage from irony, here as elsewhere in this book.

My culture is Jewish, but I am not part of normative Judaism; I decidedly do not trust in the Covenant. Those who do, or those others who accept the submission that is Islam, affirm that God is One, and that Jesus is not God, though Islam regards him as a prophetic forerunner of Allah's final messenger, Muhammad. The monotheism of Jews and of Muslims is strict and permanent.

But what precisely is the value of monotheism? Goethe, a great ironist, observed, "As students of nature we are pantheists, as poets polytheists, as moral beings monotheists." Even Freud, not a theist at all, could not divest himself of the notion that monotheism had been a moral advance upon polytheism. Freud, an atheist, remained pugnaciously Jewish; but again, why does his book translated as *Moses and Monotheism* so readily assume that a "progress in spirituality" is the proper judgment upon the movement away from polytheism? Why is "the idea of a more august God" more congenial to psychoanalysis than the labyrinthine gods of Egypt or the fierce gods of the Canaanites?

The answer appears to be *internalization,* both of authority and of fatherhood, in the Yahweh of Moses. Philip Rieff first saw this, in the late 1950s on to the mid-1960s, before the Cultural Revolution gave us the wilder Freud of Herbert Marcuse and Norman O. Brown. Now, in the early twenty-first century, a return to Rieff vindicates his insights, which were anticipated by the prophet Jeremiah, whose vision of the Covenant was that Yahweh would write the Law upon our inward parts.

When Yeshua was transformed into a theological God, first by the New Testament's Christology, and then less tentatively by Hellenistic philosophy, I cannot be clear as to what degree he was malformed, because Paul had little interest in the personality of Yeshua, and the Synoptic Gospels, the three Gospels except for John, are so frequently baffled by him. But the Yahweh of the primal text, already transmogrified by the Redactor's frequent reliance upon the Priestly Author and the Deuteronomist, all but vanishes among the great normative rabbis of the second century of the Common Era: Akiba, Ishmael, Tarphon, and their followers.

All religion, for Freud, reduces to a longing for the father, an Oedipal ambivalence that makes *The Future of an Illusion* Freud's weakest book, secretly dependent upon its misreading of Hamlet, whose actual affinities are with Montaigne and not with Christ. Freud's identification with Moses helps make *Moses and Monotheism* into one of the strongest of his more fantastic writings, where Yahweh, the warrior God, is civilized by Jewish remorse for the Jews' slaying of Moses, an event Freud imagines. That civilizing, with all its cultural discomforts, is what Freud means by "monotheism," and is an astonishing interpretation on his part. This "monotheism" actually is a repression that establishes a benign civilization, while polytheism is seen as a return to a Hobbesian state of nature, rendering life into something nasty, brutish, and short. Freud's weird transpositions work because they return us to the Yahweh of the J Writer of the Bible—the original writer of what is strongest in what we now call Genesis, Exodus, and Numbers—who bestows the Blessing of "more life, on into a time without boundaries."

Freud was obsessed with Michelangelo's sculpture of Moses, which he interpreted as showing the prophet in the act of preserving the Tablets of the Law, not of being about to cast them down in his fury of disillusion with the people's worship of the Golden Calf. Mosaic self-control is fused with Freudian sublimation of instinctual desires. Yahweh is hardly a sublimation. Is Jesus? In Mark, no, but in Matthew, as I will explain, yes. Yet it may be that the Freudian analysis of human nature is irrelevant in regard to both Yahweh and Jesus Christ, whether they are two Gods or one.

Why in particular does it matter whether or not Christianity represents a return to polytheism, as the rabbis and Muhammad in their different ways have insisted? Despite the brilliance of Christian theology, culminating in Thomas Aquinas, the Trinity is a sublimely problematic structure, not only in separating the concept of person from that of substance, but also in its positing the Holy Spirit as a crucial third with the Father and the Son, upon very little New Testament evidence. But then, I cannot recall a single passage in the Synoptic Gospels that unequivocally identifies Jesus as God: such status comes to him only in John, and clearly emerges from that Gospel's battles with those it angrily called "the Jews." Yet even in John, the status is there without the name. Yahweh and Jesus are linked for John but not fully fused.

Most Christians, in the United States as elsewhere, are not theologians, and tend to literalize doctrinal metaphors. This is hardly to be deplored, and I suspect this was true of the earliest Christians also, except that they were almost pre-theological. What is increasingly clear to me is that the emergence of Jesus-as-God pragmatically created what was to develop into Christian theology. Another way of putting this is to say that, from the start, Jesus Christ was not Yeshua but a theological rather than a human God. The mysteries of the Incarnation, and the Resurrection, have little to do with the man, Yeshua of Nazareth, and surprisingly little to do even with Paul and John, as compared with the theologians who voyaged in their wake.

YAHWEH WAS AND IS the uncanniest personification of God ever ventured by humankind, and yet early in his career he began as the warrior monarch of the people we call Israel. Whether we encounter Yahweh early or late, we confront an exuberant personality and a character so complex that unraveling it is impossible. I speak only of the Yahweh of the Hebrew Bible, and not of the God of that totally revised work, the Christian Bible, with its Old Testament and fulfilling New Testament. Historicism, be it older or newer, seems incapable of confronting the total incompatibility of Yahweh and Jesus Christ.

Jack Miles, Yahweh's Boswell, in his *God: A Biography*, depicts a Yahweh who begins in a kind of self-ignorance fused with total power and a high degree of narcissism. After various divine debacles, Miles decides, Yahweh loses interest, even in himself. Miles rightly reminds us that Yahweh, in II Samuel, promises David that Solomon will find a second father in the Lord, an adoption that sets the pattern for Jesus' asserting his sonship to God. The historical Jesus evidently insisted both upon his own authority to speak for Yahweh, and upon his own intimate relationship with his *abba* (father), and I see little difference there from some of his precursors among the charismatic prophets of Israel. The authentic difference came about with the development of the theological God, Jesus Christ, where the chain of tradition indeed is broken. Yahweh, aside from all questions of power, diverges from the gods of Canaan primarily by transcending both sexuality and death. More bluntly, Yahweh cannot be regarded as dying. Kabbalah has a vision of the erotic life of God but severely enforces the normative tradition of divine immortality. I find nothing in theological Christianity to be more difficult for me to apprehend than the conception of Jesus Christ as a dying and reviving God. The Incarnation-Atonement-Resurrection complex shatters both the Tanakh—an acronym for the three parts that make up the Hebrew Bible: the Torah (Five Books of Moses), Prophets, and Writings—and the Jewish oral tradition. I can understand Yahweh as being in eclipse, desertion, self-exile, but Yahweh's suicide is indeed beyond Hebraism.

I can object to myself that the frequently outrageous Yahweh also baffles my understanding, and that Jesus Christ is nearly as much an imaginative triumph as Yahweh is, though in a very different mode. I alternate endlessly between agnosticism and a mystical gnosis, but my Orthodox Judaic childhood lingers in me as an awe of Yahweh. No other representation of God that I have read approaches the paradoxical Yahweh of the J Writer. Perhaps I should omit "of God" from that sentence, since even Shakespeare did not invent a character whose personality is so rich in contraries. Mark's Jesus, Hamlet, Don Quixote are among the principal competitors, and so is the Homeric Odysseus transmuted into the Ulysses whose story of quest and drowning reduces Dante the Pilgrim to silence. Dennis R. MacDonald, in his *The Homeric Epics and the Gospel of Mark* (2000), argues that Mark's literary culture was more Greek than Jewish, which I find persuasive in so far as the earliest Gospel's eclecticism is thus emphasized, but a touch dubious, since Mark's God remains Yahweh. Matthew is rightly known as "the Jewish Gospel"; the Gospel of Mark is something else, though it may well have been composed just after the Temple was destroyed, and in the midst of the Roman slaughter of the Jews. Hamlet has something of the bewildering mood swings of Mark's Jesus and of Yahweh. If Don Quixote can be regarded as the protagonist of the Spanish scripture, then his enigmas also can compete with those of the Marcan Jesus and of Hamlet.

We cannot know how much of Yahweh's character and personality was invented by the J Writer, just as Mark's Jesus to some degree seems to be an original, though doubtless informed by oral tradition just as J's Yahweh was. I wonder if the author of Mark is not responsible for giving us a Jesus addicted to dark sayings. In a "cannot know" context, where what we regard as Pauline faith replaces knowledge, Mark's brilliance exploits our limits of understanding. His Jesus asserts authority, which sometimes masks wistfulness in regard to the will of Yahweh, the loving but inscrutable *abba*. Only Mark's Jesus goes through an all-night agony because his death is near. Whether, as MacDonald thinks, the suffering of Jesus emulates that of Hector at the end of the *Iliad* cannot be resolved. Jesus dies after uttering an Aramaic paraphrase of Psalm 22, an outcry of his ancestor David, a pathos distant from the Homeric variety. Doubtless the *real* Jesus existed, but he never will be found, nor need he be. *Jesus and Yahweh: The Names Divine* intends no quest. My sole purpose is to suggest that Jesus, Jesus Christ, and Yahweh are three totally incompatible personages, and to explain just how and why this is so. Of the three beings (to call them that), Yahweh troubles me the most and essentially usurps this book. His misrepresentations are endless, including by much of rabbinical tradition, and by suppressed scholarship—Christian, Judaic, and secular. He remains the West's major literary, spiritual, and ideological character, whether he is called by names as various as Kabbalah's Ein-Sof ("without end") or the Qur'an's Allah. A capricious God, this stern imp, he reminds me of an aphorism of the dark Heraclitus: "Time is a child playing draughts. The lordship is to the child."

Where shall we find the *meaning* of Yahweh, or of Jesus Christ, or of Yeshua of Nazareth? We cannot and will not find it, and "meaning" possibly is the wrong category to seek. Yahweh declares his unknowability, Jesus Christ is totally smothered beneath the massive superstructure of historical theology, and of Yeshua all we rightly can say is that he is a concave mirror, where what we see are all the distortions each of us has become. The Hebrew God, like Plato's, is a mad moralist, while Jesus Christ is a theological labyrinth, and Yeshua seems as forlorn and solitary as anyone we may know. Like Walt Whitman at the close of *Song of Myself*, Yeshua stops somewhere waiting for us.

PRELUDE: EIGHT OPENING REFLECTIONS

1. The New Covenant (Testament) is throughout marked by belated-ness in regard to the Tanakh. But the partial exceptions are the *logia*, or sayings, and parables of Jesus. Their enigmatics (to coin that) are sometimes unprecedented. Hamlet, Kierkegaard, Kafka are ironists in the wake of Jesus. All Western irony is a repetition of Jesus' enigmas/riddles, in amalgam with the ironies of Socrates.

2. Shakespearean "self-overhearing" has one source in Chaucer, but perhaps the primary Shakespearean precursor is William Tyndale's Jesus in the Geneva Bible. Internalization in Shakespeare gets beyond Jesus', though Jesus inaugurated the ever-growing inner self, developed by St. Augustine, and which Shakespeare perfected in Hamlet, after reinventing it in Falstaff.

3. The Marcan Jesus may be as close to "the real Jesus" as we can come. Matthew softens Mark. Luke is more independent of Mark, and yet also has a Jesus sometimes darker than Matthew's.

4. Doubtless the historical Jesus existed, but he can be recovered only in shards, and just a handful (or fewer) of historians are of much use in deciphering these. "Jesus: A Biography" is always an oxymoron. All theologians, from Philo to the present, are allegorists, and since allegory is irony, and demands literary insight, theologians almost always fail, Plato being the grand exception. Systematic theologians are like systematic literary critics: Paul Tillich is a modified success, Augustine is a magnificent failure, and Northrop Frye also sinks. For both Augustine and Frye, the Tanakh ceases to exist, devoured as it is by the Belated Covenant. Even Mark, who is no theologian, gives us a Jesus not wholly persuasive: his best ironies sometimes cost him his temper.

What are we to do? Well, begin by asking yourself what and who you are.

Though even most Christian scholars finally regard Jesus as Jewish, and clearly he *was* Jewish, he is now American: he is multi-everything. We may as well have a Southern Baptist or Pentecostalist or Mormon or Muslim or African or Asian Jesus as a Jewish one. His paradoxes always have been universal, but his personalism is nineteenth-century American, from the Cane Ridge Revival of 1801 all the way to the circus-like Revivalism of Charles Grandison Finney, precursor of Billy Sunday and Billy Graham. Eighty-nine percent of Americans regularly inform the Gallup pollsters that Jesus loves each of them on a personal and individual basis. That moves me perpetually to awe and to no irony whatsoever.

Can there be a Real Jesus in this era of total appropriation? His enigmas become particularly complex in the context of Second Temple Judahisms, where there was no normative doctrine, and yet for him it all began and concluded with Yahweh alone, by definition the most formidable of all ironists, ever. If there is a single principle that characterizes Jesus, it is unswerving trust in the Covenant with Yahweh. That is the essence of the Jewish religion, whether archaic, Second Temple, or the subsequent Judaism of Akiba. No Jew known at all to history can be regarded as more loyal to the Covenant than was Jesus of Nazareth. That makes it an irony-of-ironies that his followers employed him to replace the Yahweh Covenant with their New Covenant.

5. The Gospels were not intended as what we call biography, but as conversionary inspiration. In this, and in all other respects, they follow the Hebrew Bible, which paradoxically is not history in our sense, even though it remains the earliest instance of history. There is no independent account of King David exclusive of the Tanakh. Because of Josephus, we at least know that Jesus existed, though only as a peripheral figure of the century that culminated with the Roman destruction of Yahweh's Temple in the year 70 of the Common Era.

6. Endless questing for the historical Jesus has failed, in that fewer than a handful of searchers come up with more than reflections of their own faith or their own skepticism. Like Hamlet, Jesus is a mirror in which we see ourselves. Consciousness of mortality seems to allow few other options. Blame is irrelevant: where, how, can our survival be found? Jesus is to the Greek New Testament what Yahweh is to the

Hebrew Bible, or Hamlet to Shakespeare's play: the vital protagonist, the principle of apotheosis, the hope for transcendence.

Freud, reducing religion to the longing for the father, is relevant to Jesus, who called Yahweh *abba*. Since Hamlet is a skeptic, he quests for no one. Yahweh chooses Abraham and Moses and, if we submit to the Qur'an, also Muhammad. The Hebrew God cannot be said to select Jesus, except as another prophet. Pragmatically, the Son of Man fathers himself, or is the Father his own son? The American Jesus has usurped Yahweh, and may yet himself be usurped by the Holy Spirit, as we fuse into a Pentecostal nation, merging Hispanics, Asians, Africans, and Caucasian Americans into a new People of God.

7. The relation between Eros and Authority, or Love and the Law, is central to Jesus, to Paul, to Freud. But also it is crucial in Moses, in Socrates/Plato, and in *King Lear* and all Shakespeare: the *Henry IV* plays, *Hamlet, Twelfth Night* in particular. Perhaps *that* is the "meaning" of Shakespeare: the agon between Eros and the Law. Freud names the Law as Thanatos, thus oddly joining himself to Paul and to Luther. Jesus, unlike any of these, embraces both love and Torah, as scholars slowly have come to understand. Though individualistic to a degree where he refigured the messianic vision, Jesus outdoes the Pharisees (his closest rivals) in honoring the Law. His genius fused love for his father, Yahweh as *abba,* with love for the Law, oral and written, and love for his people. He remains the Jew-of-Jews, the Jew proper, triumphant over victimage while longing for the Father, and for the Kingdom where love and righteousness will be harmonized. Paul turned to the Gentiles. Jesus, as even the Synoptic Gospels make clear, certainly did not. James the Just, brother of Jesus, was his au-

thentic disciple. Scholars oddly do not see that the spirit of Jesus stands forth most clearly in the Epistle of James, composed by one of the Ebionites, or Jewish Christians, who survived the judicial murder of James and the subsequent sack of Jerusalem. Luther hated the Epistle of James, and wanted it expunged from the New Covenant. But in it we hear the voice of the Prophets in the wilderness, of Elijah and John the Baptist, and the voice of Jesus himself, for once abandoning his formidable irony.

8. The New Covenant necessarily founds itself upon a misreading of the Hebrew Bible. Yet the power of Christian translators, particularly Jerome and Tyndale, has obscured the relative weakness—aesthetic and cognitive—of the Greek New Testament in its agon with Tanakh. Even if Mark were as powerful a writer as the Yahwist, there could be no contest, since Torah (like the Qur'an) *is* God, whereas the entire argument of the Belated Testament is that a man has replaced Scripture.

PART I. JESUS

I.

WHO WAS JESUS AND WHAT
HAPPENED TO HIM?

T HERE ARE NO verifiable facts about Jesus of Nazareth. The handful in Flavius Josephus, upon which everyone relies, are suspect, because he had been Joseph ben Matthias, a leader of the Jewish Revolt, who saved his own life by fawning upon the Flavian emperors: Vespasian, Titus, Domitian. Once you have proclaimed Vespasian as the Messiah, no one again ought to believe anything you write about your own people. Josephus, a superb liar, looked on calmly as Jerusalem was captured, its Temple destroyed, its inhabitants slaughtered. Scholars assert that Josephus had little or nothing to gain by his few shreds of apparent information about the Galilean Joshua (Yeshua in Hebrew, Jesus in Greek), but so devious was the Quisling historian that his motivations, if any, are enigmatic. Josephus allows us to know that Jesus of Nazareth had Joseph and Mary (Miriam) as his parents and Jacob (James) as a brother, was baptized by John the Dipper, after which he gathered students as a wandering teacher of wisdom, and finally was crucified by the Roman satrap Pontius Pilate.

Reading and meditating upon everything available to me has made me doubt that Jesus was among the multitude of Pilate's victims. The charismatic rabbi of Nazareth was a master of evasions and ironic equivocations, a determined survivor from childhood on, once his parents had told him that, artisan as he was, his descent placed him foremost in the royal house of King David, whose progeny carried with them irrevocably the blessing of Yahweh. The firstborn of his Davidic parents, Jesus qualified for elimination by the Herodians and their Roman overlords. No more reluctant or legitimate Messiah had existed among the Jews. Heading a nationalist war against the Romans and their mercenary thugs was totally against the nature of this Jewish spiritual genius who was the legitimate king of the Jews, involuntarily and doubtless unhappily.

Jesus was not a resistance fighter, as Josephus had been, initially, until he abandoned such ferocious colleagues as Simon bar Giora and John of Gischala, leaders in the Jewish War against Rome, and saved his own life at the high cost of his integrity and of Jewish esteem. We again know nothing verifiable about what Jesus taught; we do not even know that he perhaps was born four years before the Common Era, and supposedly was crucified at what ever since is termed the chronological age of thirty-three. I suspect that, as lore has it, he had the wisdom to escape execution, and then made his way to Hellenistic northern India, the extreme limit of Alexander the Great's conquests, where some traditions place his grave. I follow Gnostic tradition in this, if only because the Gnostic sayings of Jesus in the Gospel of Thomas ring more authentically to me than the entire range of utterances attributed to him in the Synoptic Gospels and in the very late Gospel of John. There is not a sentence concerning Jesus in the entire New Testament composed by anyone who ever had met the unwilling King of the Jews, unless (and it is unlikely) the General Epistle of James truly is by James his brother, rather than by one of James's followers, the Ebionites, or "poor men," some of whom survived the holocaust of Jerusalem by departing for Pella, in Jordan, obeying James's prophetic command.

Scholars date St. Paul's epistles as forty years after the death of Jesus, with the Gospels straggling a generation or so after, and the highly Hellenistic (and quasi-Gnostic) Gospel of John at least a full century beyond the possible demise of the itinerant teacher of the poor and the outcast. There are good reasons to doubt all of this scholarly consensus, even if someone else had not been crucified in place of Jesus, as Gnostic tradition slyly suggests. James the Just, head of the Jewish Christians in Jerusalem, actually could have been the son or even the grandson of the Jacob (James) who was Jesus' own brother. Readers now, whether Christian or Jewish or Islamic, whether skeptics or believers, need to start all over again in sorting out the hidden story of the charismatic preacher who wisely decided not to become the king of the Jews, but ironically may have suffered as such by Roman hands.

2 .

QUESTS AND QUESTERS
FOR JESUS

U NLESS YOU ARE already a professional Jesus-quester, whose
sustenance, self-regard, and spiritual health depend upon your
vocation, you ought to change any plan you entertain to join that curious enterprise. Rational warnings abound; one of my favorites is the
sly irony of an essay by the immensely learned Jacob Neusner, in his
tough little book *Judaism in the Beginning of Christianity* (1984). In Chapter 4,
Neusner gives us "The Figure of Hillel: A Counterpart to the Problem
of the Historical Jesus." The admirable Hillel, a contemporary of Jesus,
was the exemplary Pharisee. Consult even an honorable volume like
The American Heritage College Dictionary (Third Edition, 1993), and you can
choose between two definitions of "Pharisee," neither of which is true
or useful, or in any way applicable to Hillel:

1. A member of an ancient Jewish sect that emphasized strict interpretation and observance of the Mosaic law.
2. A hypocritically self-righteous person.

I don't blame the dictionary's editors. Except for Paul and Mark, the New Testament endlessly and murderously slanders the Pharisees. Still, I would suggest that the first definition shed the word "strict" and substitute "sanctifying." Neusner shows us that the great Hillel, though he doubtless existed, pragmatically is an invention of rabbis of the second century of the Common Era and later. He is Judaism's own Jesus, since Yeshua of Nazareth undoubtedly existed but effectually was the invention of the New Testament. I recommend Charlotte Allen's *The Human Christ* (1998), a fair and intelligent account (by a Catholic) of the human comedy of "the search for the historical Jesus." No deprecation is intended by my Balzacian "human comedy," only my wistfulness that Balzac were with us still, to write the fictive saga that could overgo even the endlessly colorful cavalcade that Charlotte Allen and others have portrayed. A robust swarm of Christians of most denominations, very diverse Jews, secularists, and novelists good, bad, and indifferent, crowds what could have been a Balzacian masterpiece, if only we resurrected the sole French narrative magus that I, in my deep heart, love more than Stendhal, Flaubert, and Proust, though the vivacity of Stendhal, artistry of Flaubert, and wisdom of Proust are all beyond Balzac.

The incessant questing for the "true" Jesus, "historical" and uncontaminated by dogma, is akin to my perpetual inability to hold fast the Protean Vautrin, Balzac's most vivid personage in the unending procession of geniuses in *The Human Comedy*. Vautrin *is* Balzac turned homoerotic master criminal, known as "Death-Dodger" to the police and underworld alike. Each critic/reader sees his or her own Vautrin, and *every* searcher for the "historical" Jesus invariably discovers again herself or himself in Jesus. How could it be otherwise? This is hardly deplorable, particularly in the United States, where Jesus has been an American nondenominational Protestant for the last two centuries. If that *sounds* ironical, I certainly do not intend to be other than literal, and I do not disapprove of our natural tendency to hold individual conversations with a personal Jesus. I don't see that it makes Americans any gentler or more generous, but only rarely does it make them worse. Except for Shakespeare's Hamlet, I can think of no other figure as volatile as Jesus; he indeed can be all things to all women or men.

I MYSELF, on literary and spiritual grounds, prefer the Gospel of Thomas to the whole of the canonical New Testament, because that work is replete with misinformed hatred of the Jews, though composed almost entirely by Jews in flight from themselves, and desperate to ingratiate themselves with their Roman overlords and exploiters. I read Catholic scholars like Father Raymond Brown and Father John P. Meier with admiration and gratitude, and yet wonder why they will not admit how hopelessly little we actually can know about Jesus. The New Testament has been ransacked by centuries of minute scholarship, but all that labor does not result in telling us the minimal information we would demand on any parallel matter. Nobody can say who wrote the four Gospels, or precisely when and where they were composed, or what source material was relied upon. None of the writers knew Jesus, or ever heard him preach. The historian Robin Lane Fox argues otherwise, on behalf of the Gospel of John, but this is one of his rare aberrations. Even our sole source, Flavius Josephus, wonderful writer and nonstop liar, is far more interested in John the Baptist than in Jesus, who receives less than a handful of perfunctory mentions.

Ancient Jewish prophets and would-be messiahs only rarely changed into angels and never into Yahweh himself, which is why Jesus Christ (rather than Jesus of Nazareth) is a Christian and not a Jewish God. The grand exception is Enoch, who walked with Yahweh and Yahweh took him up to heaven, without the bother of dying. Up above, Enoch is Metatron, so exalted an angel that he is "the lesser Yahweh," with a throne unto himself. Rabbi Elisha ben Abuyah, most notorious of ancient Jewish *minim* (Gnostics), is reported to have ascended in order to discover that Metatron and Yahweh sat on parallel thrones. Returning, the Gnostic rabbi (known to his opponents as Acher, "the Other," or "the Stranger") proclaimed the ultimate heresy: "There are two Gods in heaven!"

In *The Human Christ* Charlotte Allen accurately reminds us that the Gospels set "Jesus as Christ above Torah." Since Torah is Yahweh, that places Christ above and beyond Yahweh, brushing all Trinitarian complexities aside. Whoever the historical Jesus was, he certainly would have rejected such blasphemy (as he does in the Qur'an). It seems absurd that Jesus, faithful to Yahweh alone, as were Hillel and Akiba, has usurped God. Yet Jesus is not the usurper, nor was St. Paul (*contra* Nietzsche and George Bernard Shaw). Like his mentor, John the Baptist, Jesus came of the Jews and *to* the Jews. Christianity falls back on saying that his own received him not, but all Christian evidence is polemical, suspect, and inadmissible in any court of law.

Academic industries do not readily disband, and there will always be quests for the *real* Jesus. No matter how responsible, I hereby wave them aside. Even the best scholars among the questers (I think first of E. P. Sanders and Father Meier) are compelled to accept as valid certain New Testament passages rather than others, while manifesting sinuous arts of explanation as to their criteria. Necessarily, results seem mixed. I am unhappy when Father Meier argues for the historicity of Judas Iscariot, who appears to me and to others—Jewish and Gentile—a transparently malevolent fiction that has helped to justify the murder of Jews for two thousand years. Sanders never darkens me, but I am puzzled when he exalts the unique charisma of Jesus on the basis of the disciples' loyalty. We ought never to forget the sociologist Max Weber's warning against the "routinization of charisma." Mere charismatics abound, and Hitler mesmerized an entire generation of Germans. Little can be argued for Jesus' uniqueness as a consequence of charisma.

And yet in writing this book, not at all a quest for me, I have been surprised both by Jesus and by Yahweh. Yahweh cannot be dismissed, though I do not trust or love him, because both absent and present he is indistinguishable from reality, be it ordinary or an intimation of transcendence. At least two different versions of Jesus, in the quasi-Gnostic Gospel of Thomas and the extraordinarily cryptic Gospel of Mark, impress me as authentic, though they are frequently antithetical to each other. Yahweh is death-our-death and life-our-life, but I do not know who Jesus of Nazareth was or is. I find him neither antithetical to Yahweh nor compatible with Yahweh: they are in diverse cosmic systems. Nothing about Yahweh is Greek: Homer, Plato, Aristotle, the Stoics, and the Epicureans all are alien to him. Jesus, like his contemporary Hillel and like Akiba a century later, emerges from a Hellenized Jewry, though the extent of its contamination by Greek modes is disputed and disputable.

Yahweh is unknowable, however deeply we read in Torah and Talmud, and in Kabbalah. Is Jesus—as contrasted with the Jesus Christ of theology—knowable? The American Jesus is known intimately, as friend and comforter, by tens of millions. The American Jesus can be more Pauline than Gospel-oriented: the Southern Baptist moderates found themselves upon the Epistle to the Romans. Pentecostalists, burgeoning throughout the United States, pragmatically displace Jesus by their kinetic reliance upon the Holy Spirit. Mormons, most American and surprising of orientations, regard Joseph Smith's (or the Angel Moroni's) Book of Mormon as Another Testament of Jesus Christ, and yet have more surprising scriptures that their current hierarchy evades in Smith's *The Pearl of Great Price* and his *Doctrines and Covenants.* By now, Joseph Smith has ascended and transmuted into Enoch, and perhaps also into the greatest of the angels, Metatron or the Lesser Yahweh, a Kabbalistic vision. I do not apprehend much of this radiating now out of Salt Lake City, but Joseph Smith and Brigham Young believed in the doctrine that Adam and God ultimately were the same person. The human and the divine interpenetrate in Joseph Smith's vision far more radically than in the Catholic Church's insistence that Christ was both "true man" and "true God." It is because American Religionists (including elite spirits like Emerson and Whitman) believed that the best and oldest parts of them were not natural but divine that Jesus can be conversed with so freely and so fully by many among us. That may well not be the "historical Jesus" of the scholarly questers, but he seems to me quite close to the "living Jesus" who speaks in the Gospel of Thomas.

3.

THE DARK SPEAKING
OF JESUS

My CONCERNS in this book are with the personality, character, and self-recognitions of Yahweh and of Jesus. With Jesus, these are revealed only darkly in what we are told were his own words, which are frequently enigmatic, and perhaps more ambivalent even than they are ambiguous.

We do not know how many languages Jesus spoke: Aramaic certainly, and some demotic Greek probably. Hebrew he evidently could read, and perhaps speak. Father John P. Meier, the author of three magisterial volumes under the somewhat misleading title *A Marginal Jew* (with a much-needed fourth volume to come), accurately terms Jesus "a Jewish genius." One can go further: Jesus was the greatest of Jewish geniuses. It is as though the Yahwist or J Writer somehow was fused with King David, with the Prophets from Amos through Malachi, with the Wisdom authors of Job and Koheleth (Ecclesiastes), with the sages from Hillel through Akiba, and with the long sequence that goes from Maimonides through Spinoza on to Freud and Kafka. Jesus is the Jewish Socrates, and surpasses Plato's mentor as the supreme master of dark wisdom.

Love, rather than irony, is what believers seek and find in Jesus. They may be in the right, for his could be more an ironic love than a loving irony. I myself, more a knower than a believer of any sort, am culturally Jewish. Nevertheless I do not trust in the Covenant, as Jesus did. From St. Paul onward, believers have seen Jesus as the inventor of a New Covenant, but they may have confused the messenger with the message.

Jesus confronts us, nonbelievers and believers alike, with an array of enigmas. Yet how could it be otherwise? Islam accepts Muhammad as the Seal of the Prophets, but grants Jesus a unique status among the precursors of the ultimate, definitive prophet in a line that stems from Abraham. Jews have a negative relationship to Christ, but not necessarily to Jesus, who is scarcely responsible for what supposed Christianity has done in his name. Kierkegaard, another master of irony (which he called "indirect communication"), remarked in his *Judge for Yourself!*: "Christianity has completely conquered—that is, it is abolished!" Evidently, the Danish sage meant that you could become a Christian only in opposition to the established order.

This book disputes Christendom's persuasion that Jesus intended to found what became the faith of St. Paul. But I venture no quarrel with Jesus, who stood for "Yahweh alone," while implying capacious comprehension of the hazards of such a stance. When the recalcitrant Moses, in the J Writer's text, plaintively asks the name of the God who is sending him down into Egypt, Yahweh massively proclaims, *Ehyeh asher ehyeh.* The traditional rendering is "I Am That I Am," which I explicate as "I will be present whenever and wherever I will be present."

The terrible irony of Yahweh's pun on his own name is that the opposite also is implied: "And I will be absent whenever and wherever I will be absent," including at the destructions of his Temple, at the German death camps, at Golgotha.

William Tyndale, Protestant martyr and greatest of Bible translators (at least since St. Jerome), rendered what we read in the Authorized Version as St. Paul's "For now we see through a glass darkly" even more powerfully: "Now we see in a glass even in a dark speaking." "Dark speaking" interprets the Greek for "enigma." Albert Schweitzer, preaching in 1905, said, "The glorified body of Jesus is to be found in his sayings." But there is a difficulty Jesus never intended: *which are his authentic sayings?* Most scholars possess inward criteria for such authenticity, and voting among and by them does not persuade me. Each of us, particularly in the United States, has her or his own Jesus. Mine goes back to childhood, when I first read the Gospels in a Yiddish version left at the door of our Bronx apartment by a missionary. A Yiddish New Testament (I still have it) constitutes its own irony, reflecting two millennia of Jewish stubbornness, yet the translation is both skilled and severe. I recall also taking a course with Professor Friedrich Solmsen in the Greek New Testament at Cornell, and have just reread that text after fifty-five years, somewhat startled at my angry marginal notes, clustered mostly in Paul and the Gospel of John. If your first language, your mother tongue, was Yiddish, then you have had an apt preparation to receive the dark sayings of Jesus. Born in my parents' Eastern Europe, Jesus would have spoken Yiddish, and would probably have been martyred not by the Romans but by the Germans.

I am dubious about the phrase "the Jewish-Christian tradition."

Now it refers to a particular sociopolitical phenomenon, and seems part of the alliance between the United States and Israel. In this book it means the stance of James the Just, brother of Jesus, and the rest of his family and first followers, who only grudgingly accepted Paul's mission to the Gentiles, and then eventually were absorbed into the Imperial Church of Constantine or into Islam.

(2)

I have already written that Jesus' words are frequently enigmatic. What is an enigma? It can be a verbal riddle, or a puzzling thing, or an inexplicable person. Jesus speaks the first almost invariably, his actions give us the second, and he himself is the third. The word "enigma" goes back from Latin to Greek, and has an ultimate base in a Greek word meaning "fable."

Whether in aphorisms or in parables, Jesus speaks riddles. He is the poet of the riddle, anticipating Dante, Shakespeare, Cervantes, John Donne, and even Lewis Carroll and James Joyce, as well as Kierkegaard, Emerson, Nietzsche, Kafka, and many others in the literary and spiritual tradition of the West. To make some progress with understanding the dark speaking of Jesus, I need to define "riddle," "aphorism," and "parable" as best I can:

1. RIDDLE

The word "riddle" goes back to a Germanic base meaning "a question or opinion that needs ingenuity in conjecturing an answer or counterstatement." Another meaning is "a perplexity or mystery," and yet another, "an inexplicable person, like Jesus or the fictive Hamlet."

2. APHORISM

This word goes from French through Latin to the Greek for "defining" or "setting a horizon." Originally the noun meant a pithy statement by a classical writer or orator but became any maxim or condensed precept.

3. PARABLE

The noun "parable" comes through French from the Latin for "comparison," thus leading to such meanings as "similitude," "proverb," and "mystical saying," but is primarily an imagined short narrative whose lesson or point is spiritually moral.

The riddles of Jesus tend to turn upon the question of just who Jesus is. Sometimes he utters them as charms against Satan. Charms are riddles turned pragmatic, magical if only because they sometimes work. Their function for Jesus is to further his enormous venture in self-identification. *We* discover our true selves receding further the more we quest to find them. The apotheosis of Jesus is that his authentic identity may have proved fatal, since he could well have been the authentic Davidic heir to the Kingdom of Israel and Judah, rather than to a realm not of this world. Since the family of Herod had assumed all royal authority, any authentic descendant of David always was in danger. Shakespeare's Hamlet, heir to Denmark, seems to me shadowed by William Tyndale's Jesus, a recognition in which I follow David

Daniell, the biographer of the heroic, martyred Protestant translator and authentic inventor of an English prose style austerely sublime.

But why did Jesus frequently speak in riddles? His parables follow and perfect Hebrew tradition; Yahweh himself, throughout the J Writer's text, delights in riddling puns, unanswerably rhetorical questions, and fiercely playful outbursts that edge upon a frightening fury. "Like father, like son," a believer aptly could reply. Whoever wrote Mark, the first Gospel to be composed, was such a believer, and went back to Yahweh at the God's uncanniest in order to suggest something of the secret of Jesus.

Paul and the other three Gospel authors (or traditions) have and partly deserve their literary admirers, yet Mark stands by itself as the enigma-of-enigmas, endlessly resistant to analysis. Frank Kermode's *The Genesis of Secrecy* (1979) remains the most brilliant endeavor to ambush the ambiguities of Mark. Rereading Kermode's book, after a quarter century, I am stimulated to augment his pioneer analysis by swerving from it into surmise as to the psychology of Jesus. Even the most refined of Freudian psychosexual speculations seem to me irrelevant in regard to Jesus, because his relation both to his mother and to his putative father is remarkably disengaged; my psychologizing here will therefore owe more to William James than to Sigmund Freud, though I consider the founder of psychoanalysis the prime incarnation of Jewish genius since Jesus himself. With a consciousness so devoted to Yahweh alone, the varieties of religious experience can be more revelatory than the vicissitudes of the psychosexual drive.

My late friend Hans Frei concluded his *The Identity of Jesus Christ* (1975) by cautioning us that we always will be at a distance from Jesus "because he lives to God—not to time." Kierkegaard made the same observation but with superb doubleness, remarking that disciples contemporary with Jesus received his love without understanding it, since Jesus alone understands himself perfectly. Disputing Kierkegaard is dangerous, and the perplexities of Jesus are even more dangerous.

Another late friend, Edward Shils, in his *Tradition* (1981), followed Max Weber by finding in Jesus the supreme charismatic:

> It was Jesus' prophetic or charismatic imagination which determined his accomplishment. He had the gift of arousing in others an acknowledgment or attribution of charismatic qualities. He did this by the originality of his message and his own belief in his originality. He had to have the tradition as his point of departure; he had to have an audience which had the same tradition as its point of departure. In that sense he was continuing and developing the tradition, but so for that matter were the rabbis. He developed it in a different and more original way and his message found a reception far beyond Palestine and the Jews. The receptiveness of this wider body of converts, who were won over from paganism and not just from Judaism, might have been a result of the changes in circumstances and of the relative weakness of the traditions of paganism in confrontation with a more highly developed body of religious thought.

But did Jesus believe in the *originality* of his message? Was it not the same message of his mentor, John the Baptist? And how different actually was it from the stance of Hillel? To what degree can we distinguish between the charismatic and his proclamations?

JESUS, to most Americans, of whatever origin or denomination, is
both unique and universal. Has he taken the place once held by God
the Father? If so, then the American Religion would evade Freud's reduction of all religion to the longing for the father. For a while now, I
have rejected Marx's notion that religion was the opiate of the people.
In the United States it is rather the people's poetry, both bad and
good. Still, this remains the Age of the American Jesus, omnipresent
and intensely personal. Most people scarcely can read anymore, and
much of the New Testament is difficult, relying as it does upon incessant reference to and "fulfillment" of the Hebrew Bible, itself not the
simplest of verbal structures. Vast and magnificent, the Tanakh
hardly seems "the Old Testament," led in Roman triumph by its re-
sentful child, "the New Testament." Yet the unpredictable and abrupt
Jesus of the Gospel of Mark is smoothly consistent when compared
with the Yahweh of the oldest strand of Genesis, Exodus, and Numbers. Shakespeare's King Lear is to Hamlet what the J Writer's Yahweh
is to Mark's Jesus.

Where shall we locate the meanings of Mark's Jesus? Kermode
shrewdly admired Mark's narrative for concealing at least as much as
it discloses, engendering secrecy even as it cries out the Good News.
Mark's Jesus is not much interested in Gentiles, and even among Jews
he seeks only a saving remnant. So complex is his stance as a teacher
that he could not survive institutional review in the United States of
today, whether academic or denominational. This Jesus follows Isaiah
by excluding those who cannot hear his truths or see his visions with
him. An angry prophet like Elijah or John the Baptist is too simple a

precursor for Jesus to follow. He turns to Isaiah, the Plato among the prophets, as his authentic forerunner.

The Gospel of Mark 4:11–12 gives us Jesus paraphrasing Isaiah 6:9–10, with Mark not identifying the source. Matthew, however, acknowledges it by direct quotation. Kermode interprets this difference as an unhappiness in Matthew with "the gloomy ferocity of Mark's Jesus." One might also call Mark's Jesus outrageous in *his* fury. I cite Isaiah here from the Jewish Publication Society's Tanakh, and Mark from the Revised Standard Version:

> Then I heard the voice of my Lord saying, "Whom shall I send? Who will go for us?" And I said, "Here am I; send me." And He said, "Go, say to that people:
>> 'Hear, indeed, but do not understand;
>> See, indeed, but do not grasp.'
>> Dull that people's mind,
>> Stop its ears,
>> And seal its eyes—
>> Lest, seeing with its eyes
>> And hearing with its ears,
>> It also grasp with its mind,
>> And repent and save itself."
>
> ISAIAH 6:8–10

> And he said to them, "To you has been given the secret of the kingdom of God, but for those outside everything comes in parables; in order that 'they may indeed look, but not perceive, and may indeed listen, but not understand; so that they may not turn again and be forgiven.'"
>
> MARK 4:11–12

Yahweh's irony is not uncharacteristic of him, nor is that of Jesus.
Do these ironies clash? That of Jesus alludes to Isaiah 6:9–10, though
its shock is hardly staled by the repetition, any more than Robert
Frost's citation of Mark, in his great poem "Directive," is lessened in
impact by its biblical precursors:

> I have kept hidden in the instep arch
> Of an old cedar at the waterside
> A broken drinking goblet like the Grail
> Under a spell so the wrong ones can't find it,
> So can't get saved, as Saint Mark says they mustn't.

In a later chapter, on Mark's Gospel, I will return to these perplexities.

(3)

Jesus, in his reliance upon riddles, both extends and alters the tonali-
ties of the oral tradition of his people. Here St. Paul has been the worst
of all possible guides, with his "The letter kills, but the spirit gives life"
(II Corinthians 3:6). That is antithetical to Jesus of Nazareth, who tells
us that "not an iota, not a dot, will pass from the law until all is accomplished" (Matthew 5:18). Matthew, though evidently Jewish (like
Mark, but not Luke), hardly gives us an antinomian Jesus, though his
protagonist is largely free of the fury of Mark's hero, who also remained
stubbornly a Galilean devoted to Yahweh alone. There are many versions of Jesus outside the canonical New Testament, but this, to me,

seems far less interesting than that there are at least seven Jesuses in the book of the New Covenant, embedded in the four Gospels, in Paul, in the Epistle of James, the brother of Jesus, and in the Apocalypse. The Jesus of the Acts of the Apostles is so similar to Luke's that one easily accepts the scholarly judgment that the same author-editor or editors compiled them both. Though my personal distaste for Paul and the violently anti-Jewish Gospel of John is considerable, I will brood on their Jesuses also, since his personality, character, and consciousness of identity scarcely can be discerned without some resort to Paul and to John.

The first observation that I am moved to make is that all of the New Testament is obsessed with its anxious relationship to the Law and the Prophets, and seeks to resolve a complex anguish resulting from that overwhelming influence, by the strongest and most successful creative misreading in all of textual history. The Qur'an is the nearest rival I know. Nothing in secular literature, not even Shakespeare's triumph over all of anteriority, quite matches Paul and his successors in their intricate endeavor that transformed the Hebrew Bible, strongest of texts except for Shakespeare, into "the Old Testament." The New Testament is a remarkable (though uneven) literary achievement, but no secular reader (who knows how to read) could judge it to be of the aesthetic eminence of almost all of the Hebrew Bible (excluding Leviticus and the non-Yahwistic parts of Numbers). William Faulkner expressed a persuasive preference for the immensely varied stories of the Hebrew Bible as compared with the Greek New Testament, which strives to tell one story and one story only.

Though all of Christian theology, as well as the formidable Dante and his devoted exegetes, avers otherwise, nevertheless no later text ever has "fulfilled" an earlier one, or even "corrected" it. Plato's *Republic* battles Homer's *Iliad,* and Plato gloriously is defeated. Joyce's *Ulysses* boldly engages both Homer's *Odyssey* and Shakespeare's *Hamlet,* and sublimely loses. Historically, both the New Testament and the Qur'an have pragmatically eclipsed the Hebrew Bible, but these successes are neither aesthetic nor necessarily spiritual, and Yahweh may not yet have spoken his final word upon this matter. We all know that history rides with the big battalions and, for a time, favors those who win the big wars, but history is an ironist almost of Jesus' genius, and the signs of an apocalyptic war between Christendom (to call it that) and Islam are now omnipresent.

(4)

Seven versions of Jesus could be considered in their likely order of chronological composition: Paul, Mark, Matthew, Luke and the Acts, James, John, and the Apocalypse. I suggest that the temporal frame is somewhat irrelevant, since some of these visions of Jesus owe little or nothing to their forerunners. James the Just, austerely sublime brother of Jesus, is wholly independent, because his remarkable letter relies upon a wholly implicit Christ, whose Good News is already grasped by his auditors, the "letter" actually constituting an Ebionite, or Jewish-Christian, sermon. Though scholars date the Epistle of James near the end of the first century, I suspect it was composed less than a decade after the Roman destruction of Jerusalem and the Temple. Addressed rather clearly to Hebrew Christians, as I have noted, it may well be the work of an actual disciple of James. If so, this particular follower of James the Just wrote a remarkably good Greek style, and thus could have emerged from Alexandrian Jewry and later come into James's company.

James was slain sometime between 62 and 67 C.E. I cannot care much about who wrote his Epistle, in what place or when, because the stance and aura of Jewish Christianity has never been better exemplified than in this eloquent sermon. And yet James was revered by so wide an array of groups, from Gnostics to Gentile Christians, that the Epistle need not have been written by anyone who actually knew the saintly sage.

There are no explicit references to Jesus (or to Paul) in the Epistle of James, though Jesus is directly echoed in 2:8, but the example of Jesus is presupposed throughout. Since there is an overt polemic against Paul, I am not impressed when scholars argue that James and Paul subtly can be reconciled. Martin Luther's anti-Semitic diatribe against James counts far more: he reacted with fury to the Epistle's "a man is justified by works and not by faith alone" (2:24), a manifest repudiation of Paul's "a man is justified by faith and not by works" (Romans 3:28).

My concern here is with the Epistle's internalized vision of Jesus, to whom James had returned after Jesus' Resurrection and thus reconciled with his extraordinary brother. Oral tradition, presumably Ebionite, may govern the Jesus we can peer at between the sentences of the sermon. This Jesus is a prophet in the great procession that began with Amos in the Tanakh, possibly eight centuries before the Common Era. In Amos, Yahweh declaims:

> I loathe, I spurn your festivals,
> I am not appeased by your solemn assemblies.
> If you offer me burnt offerings—or your meal offerings—
> I will not accept them;
> I will pay no heed
> To your gifts of fatlings.
> Spare me the sounds of your hymns,
> And let me not hear the music of your lutes.
> But let justice well up like water,
> Righteousness like an unfailing stream.
>
> 5:21–24

The Jewish Publication Society translation, accurate and spirited, lacks the eloquence of the Authorized Version:

> But let judgment run down as water, and righteousness as a mighty river.

Judgment and righteousness are at the center of James, and of his Jesus:

> Behold, the wages of the laborers who mowed your fields, which you kept back by fraud, cry out; and the cries of the harvesters have reached the ears of the Lord of Hosts.
>
> 5:4

Jesus promised the kingdom to the poor, and James calls them the "heirs" of the coming of the kingdom when the risen Lord returns. "Wisdom" is the gift of God that James beseeches, and for him and Jesus the essence of the Law is Leviticus 19:18:

> You shall not take vengeance or bear a grudge against your country-
> men. Love your fellow as yourself: I am the Lord.

4·

THE BELATED TESTAMENT

READING STRAIGHT THROUGH the New Testament, in its canonical ordering, is for me a unique experience, both literary and spiritual. Christian Scripture has a relationship to the Hebrew Bible very unlike that of Vergil to Homer, or Shakespeare to Chaucer and to the English Bible. Vergil knew Lucretius and other Roman works, and a wide range of Greek literature, including Hellenistic "modernists," while Shakespeare was eclectic, a magpie collecting riches from Ovid to Christopher Marlowe. But Yeshua of Nazareth was preoccupied with the Teaching and the Prophets, the principal texts of his own people. His followers, whether Jewish or Gentile Christians, were in no position to cast off the writings that had nurtured their Lord Jesus Christ. And yet increasingly their stance in regard to the Hebrew Scriptures was one of acute ambivalence.

This unsteady veering between love and hatred of "the Jews" within the Gospels has inspired a long history of violence. Paul, a Pharisee by training, is mostly free of the virulent intensities of John, and yet he inaugurated the incessant misreadings of the Jewish Bible that culminated in John. For Paul, the Resurrection, or Christ event, proclaimed the death of Torah: since the end of all existence was very near, moral law became irrelevant. Two thousand years after Paul, it is a little bewildering to absorb what cannot be termed a mere delay in finalities. The Resurrection and the Parousia (Second Coming) appear to exist in quite different worlds, from the perspective of the twenty-first century of the Common Era.

Donald Akenson emphasizes the paradox that Christianity was invented in the first century c.e., *before* Rabbinical Judaism developed in the second century: Paul precedes Akiba. The normative sages of the second century have no direct continuity with the Pharisees, or at least we lack evidence that links them. Yet the Mishnah, the Rabbinical codification of the Oral Law, is anything but belated, and has no ambivalence toward the Torah, or Written Law, which it massively completes. Akiba made the terrible mistake of proclaiming the heroic warrior Bar Kochba as Messiah, and the rebellion they led together against Rome from 132 to 135 c.e. destroyed more Jews than had died sixty years earlier, when the Temple was obliterated, though at least many of them died fighting. The Emperor Hadrian, appalled at his legions' losses in battle, announced his victory in a message to the Roman Senate that omitted the usual formula: "The Emperor and the Army are well." Akiba or Jesus Christ? Judaism, by the fourth century c.e., exchanged Roman pagan enemies for Roman Christian oppressors.

As a critic I have learned to rely upon the admonition that opens Emerson's first volume of *Essays:* there is no history, only biography;

and upon his allied apprehension that our prayers are diseases of the will and our creeds diseases of the intellect. The New Testament is myth and faith, not a factual chronicle, and the writings of the untrustworthy Josephus have been falsified by Christian redactors. Jesus lacks both history and biography, and which of his sayings and teachings are authentic cannot be known. If you accept the Incarnation, none of this matters. Judaism after all is equally unreliable: did the Exodus actually happen? Christ's miracles, like Yahweh's, persuade only the persuaded.

I can think of only a handful or less of my contemporaries who are inwardly free to write about ancient religious texts without manifesting their own spiritual persuasions: Donald Harman Akenson, Robin Lane Fox, F. E. Peters would be among them. The most trustworthy authorities on Jesus, as I have mentioned, seem to me John P. Meier and E. P. Sanders, respectively Catholic and Protestant, but as believers they necessarily share in some blindness, particularly in the hope that somehow the New Testament can reveal the actual or historical Jesus.

No other scholar is as clarifying on that tired old horse "the Quest for the Historical Jesus" as Akenson. As he remarks, with perfect confidence, there indeed was a Yeshua of Nazareth who eventually was transformed into Jesus the Christ by his believers. Unfortunately, almost everything we are told about him is in the canonical New Testament, or in extracanonical Christian texts. From the Jewish historian Josephus, we know only that Yeshua was crucified by order of Pontius Pilate, that his brother James the Just later was stoned to death by order of the Jewish Sanhedrin, and that John the Baptist, Yeshua's forerunner, was executed by the Herodians.

Akenson has a higher aesthetic judgment of the unity of the New Testament than I am able to achieve. For him, it is a single source, and from it we can recover a glimpse or two of Yeshua of Nazareth. After many readings of the New Testament and its best scholars, regretfully I myself have not recovered a single clear glimpse. I guess, with Akenson, that Yeshua was a Pharisee, since ironically that accounts for the anti-Pharisaic fury of the New Testament, which needs to distinguish this particular Pharisee from all the others. Except for that, I have no other surmise.

The central procedure of the New Testament is the conversion of the Hebrew Bible into the Old Testament, so as to abrogate any stigma of belatedness that might be assigned to the New Covenant, when contrasted with the "Old" Covenant. A comparison to the Qur'an is instructive. Muhammad constantly refers to biblical personages and stories, which evidently were familiar to the auditors of his recitation. Frequently these references seem skewed to us, since they perhaps were based upon Jewish-Christian sources we no longer possess. All of these evocations of old stories are freestyle and not particularly programmatic. Though the Jews and Christians were "people of the Book," *that* book was neither the Tanakh nor the New Testament. Whatever it may have been, it induced no anxiety in Muhammad, who does not rely upon these earlier beliefs to provide a design for the contours of Allah's discourse. The Seal of the Prophets corrects earlier visions while passing them by, but they are source material and not guidance for him.

The canonical New Testament writers have an altogether different relation to the Torah and the Prophets, since their Messiah is for them

the fulfillment both of the Genesis-to-Kings narrative melded together in Babylon, and all the messengers from Moses through Elijah
to Malachi. Rearranging the Tanakh's ordering, so that it ends with
Malachi and not with II Chronicles, is only their opening revision of
Scripture. The New Testament is designed as a prism through which
its precursor text is to be read, revised, and interpreted. Paul is particularly adept at this reworking, but all who come after him, down to
the authors of Hebrews and Revelation, are superbly gifted in the arts
of usurpation, reversal, and appropriation. However one judges the
New Testament, whether as literature or as spirituality, it is historically the most totally successful makeover ever accomplished. Since
Christians worldwide now outnumber Jews by more than a thousand
to one, you could assert (if you wished) that the New Testament
rescued the Hebrew Bible, but you would be mistaken. Christians
have saved *their* Old Testament, to borrow an emphasis from Jaroslav
Pelikan.

The Genesis-to-Kings sequence is a narrative fiction masking as
history. After the disasters of the Jewish War and of the Bar Kochba rebellion, the Jews abandoned narrative and history, as Yosef Yeru-
shalmi eloquently demonstrated in *Zakhor,* his excursus concerning
Judaic memory. Rabbinical literature, however impressive, particularly in the Babylonian Talmud, does not resemble the Tanakh. What
is now termed Judaism has much more to do with postbiblical writings. The New Testament usurpation of the Hebrew Bible constituted
a kind of trauma that prevails among Jewry. Commentary asserted itself over narrative. In the twentieth century, I would have chosen
Kafka, Freud, and Gershom Scholem as the major figures in Jewish

literary culture, and even Kafka was more a parabolist than a narrator. Now, in whatever particle of the new century I remain here to see, it is not yet clear whether *our* Kafka, Philip Roth, is primarily exegete or storyteller.

AT SEVENTY-FOUR, I continue my own quest to resolve some of the enigmas of the influence process, whether in imaginative literature or between religious texts. This book culminates for me what began half my lifetime ago, on my thirty-seventh birthday, when I woke up from a nightmare to begin writing an essay called "The Covering Cherub or Poetic Influence." This was published six years later, much revised, as the opening chapter of a short book called *The Anxiety of Influence* (1973). Though I did not include it in the final book, I remember composing a section on the New Testament's anxiety of influence in regard to the Hebrew Bible, which is the subject of this chapter, "The Belated Testament."

I have learned that my idea, the anxiety of influence, is very easily misunderstood, which is natural, since I base the notion on the process of "misreading," by which I do not intend dyslexia. Later works misread earlier ones; when the misreading is strong enough to be eloquent, coherent, and persuasive to many, then it will endure, and sometimes prevail. The New Testament frequently is a strong misreading of the Hebrew Bible, and certainly it has persuaded multitudes. Jack Miles, in his provocative *God: A Biography,* gives a useful formula for understanding the New Testament's transformation of the Tanakh into its Old Testament, naming it "the strongest reading of any classic in literary history." I do not agree with the exuberant

Akenson that the New Testament approaches the aesthetic eminence of the Tanakh, but still I acknowledge extraordinary if intermittent splendors in Paul and Mark, and alas throughout the Gospel of John. Many of these, however, are the creation of William Tyndale, the only true rival of Shakespeare, Chaucer, and Walt Whitman as the richest author in the English language. Tyndale's New Testament is the staple of the Authorized Version, or King James Bible, and abides (somewhat diminished) in the Revised Standard Version. Only Shakespeare's prose is capable of surviving comparison with Tyndale's, and part of my passion for the magnificent Sir John Falstaff stems from the Fat Knight's boisterous parodies of Tyndale's style.

Influence is a kind of *influenza,* a contamination once thought to pour in upon us from the stars. Mark's influenza was caught by him from the J Writer, or Yahwist; Paul's and John's cases stem from the Law and the Prophets alike. The great critic Northrop Frye (who had contaminated me) remarked to me that whether a later reader experienced such an effect was entirely a matter of temperament and circumstances. With amiable disloyalty I answered that influence anxiety was not primarily an effect in an individual, but rather the relation of one work of literature to another. Therefore the anxiety of influence is the result, and not the cause, of a strong misreading. With that, we parted (intellectually) forever, though in old age I appreciate the irony that my criticism is to his as the New Testament is to the Tanakh, which is spiritually the paradoxical reverse of our spiritual preferences.

The New Testament accomplishes its appropriation by means of its drastic reordering of the Tanakh. Here is the original sequence of the Tanakh, contrasted with the Christian Old Testament:

OLD TESTAMENT	TANAKH
Genesis	Genesis
Exodus	Exodus
Leviticus	Leviticus
Numbers	Numbers
Deuteronomy	Deuteronomy
Joshua	Joshua
Judges	Judges
Ruth	
I Samuel	I Samuel
II Samuel	II Samuel
Kings	Kings
	Isaiah
	Jeremiah
	Ezekiel
	Twelve Minor Prophets
I Chronicles	Psalms
II Chronicles	Proverbs
Ezra	Job
Nehemiah	
Tobit	
Judith	
Esther	Song of Songs
Maccabees	Ruth
Job	Lamentations
Psalms	Ecclesiastes
Proverbs	Esther
Ecclesiastes	Daniel

Song of Songs	Ezra
Wisdom	Nehemiah
Ecclesiasticus (Sirach)	I Chronicles
Isaiah	II Chronicles
Jeremiah	
Lamentations	
Baruch	
Ezekiel	
Daniel	
Twelve Minor Prophets	

The King James Bible, with which readers of this book are likely to be most familiar, departs from the Tanakh's order initially by inserting Ruth between Judges and I Samuel, perhaps because as the ancestress of David, she is the remote ancestress also of Jesus. Then, in a major change, it follows Kings with Chronicles, Ezra, Nehemiah, Esther, Job, Psalms, Proverbs, Ecclesiastes, and Solomon's Song, before proceeding to the major prophets Isaiah and Jeremiah, whose Lamentations are then inserted before Ezekiel. Then comes Daniel, given the status of a major prophet, and then all is concluded with the grouping of the Twelve Minor Prophets, from Hosea through Malachi.

Aside from the inclusion of the apocryphal works, the crucial Christian revisions are its elevation of Daniel and the difference in endings, from II Chronicles to Malachi, the last of the Twelve Minor Prophets:

And in the first year of King Cyrus of Persia, when the word of the Lord spoken by Jeremiah was fulfilled, the Lord roused the spirit of

King Cyrus of Persia to issue a proclamation throughout his realm by word of mouth and in writing, as follows: "Thus said King Cyrus of Persia: the Lord God of Heaven has given me all the kingdoms of the earth, and has charged me with building Him a House in Jerusalem, which is in Judah. Any one of you of all His people, the Lord his God be with him and let him go up."

II CHRONICLES 36:22–23

The Tanakh's conclusion is the heartening exhortation to "go up" to Jerusalem to rebuild Yahweh's Temple. (Of course, today a restored Temple would be a universal catastrophe, since Al Aksa Mosque occupies the sacred site, and must not be removed.) In order to lead into the three opening chapters of the Gospel of Matthew, the Christian Old Testament concludes with Malachi, "the Messenger," proclaiming Elijah's return (as John the Baptist):

Behold, I will send you Elijah the prophet before the coming of the great and dreadful day of the Lord:

And he shall turn the heart of the fathers to the children, and the heart of the children to their fathers, lest I come and smite the earth with a curse.

MALACHI 4:5–6

Belated Testament as truly it is, the New Covenant is most intense in the belated Gospel of John, which I find both aesthetically strong and spiritually appalling, even setting aside its vehement Jewish self-hatred, or Christian anti-Semitism. If the New Testament triumphed in the Roman mode, and it did under Constantine, then the captive led in procession was the Tanakh, reduced to slavery as the Old Testament. All subsequent Jewish history, until the founding more than half a century ago of the State of Israel, testifies to the human consequences of that textual slavery.

5.

ST. PAUL

PAULUS (he never calls himself Saul in his letters) identified himself as a Jew from Tarsus, in Cilicia, where he was born sometime between 5 and 10 C.E. Probably a Roman citizen by birth, he presumably spoke Greek as a child, yet could read Hebrew and speak Aramaic, since he was a Pharisee. Acts 22:3 asserts that Paul, presumably as a young man, studied in Jerusalem with the great sage Gamaliel the Elder, which may have been true.

By his own boast, Paul began his public activity as a leader of violence against Jewish Christians, until his famous encounter with the voice of the resurrected Christ on the road to Damascus. Accepting the call to be an apostle of a figure whom he had never met, Paul devoted the remainder of his life to the conversion of Gentiles to his own understanding of the New Covenant. Sometime after the summer of 64 C.E., he was martyred in Nero's Rome, after a thirty-year apostolic labor.

There are seven indisputable letters of Paul in the New Testament, composed from 51 through 62 (or so), which makes them the earliest Christian writings we possess. If you add the half-dozen letters attributed to him by his disciples, and the larger part of Luke's Book of Acts, where Paul is the hero, then about a third of the New Testament is Pauline. Between his priority, his centrality in the text, and his reinvention of much of Christianity, Paul is its crucial founder. Yeshua of Nazareth, who died still trusting in the Covenant with Yahweh, cannot be regarded as the inaugurator of a new faith.

The vehemence and violence of the Apostle's personality are revealed throughout his letters, which mostly are argued against Jewish Christians, rather than against Jews and Judaism. Pharisees, the hated opponents in Matthew, are not a target for Paul. He does not regard them as peculiarly prone to sin nor, as their student, does he think of himself in that way.

Wayne Meeks, whose apprehension of Paul subtly allows for the Apostle's enigmatic and Protean nature, nevertheless startles me by defending the Apostle's "waging of peace." James the Just of Jerusalem hardly would have agreed, and a close rereading of Paul does not divulge an irenic temperament. Paul's Epistle to the Galatians opposes a group that scholarship cannot quite identify, but they must have winced as they read the catalogue of their works: "immorality, impurity, licentiousness, idolatry, sorcery, enmity, strife, jealousy, anger, selfishness, dissension, party spirit, envy, drunkenness, carousing, and the like." Not much has changed.

Can anyone *like* Paul? Only my dedicatee, Donald Akenson, shows a wry affection for the Apostle in *Saint Saul* (2000), pointing out accurately that Jesus Christ, in the Gospels, has become a divinity, while Paul "is a jagged, flawed, and therefore totally convincing human being." Writing in 1913, in the Preface to his *Androcles and the Lion,* George Bernard Shaw compared Paul to Karl Marx, finding in each a fantastic builder of error that exiled all moral responsibility. That seems about right to me.

(2)

Paul is more an agitator than a mystical theologian, let alone a systematic thinker. His Yahweh shrinks to God the Father, and pragmatically has little function except in relation to the Son. Since Paul's Christ is as cut off from any historical Jesus as his God the Father is from Yahweh, there is a curious emptiness in Pauline doctrine. It is not an accident that Paul emphasizes the *kenosis,* the self-emptying-out of the divine that the Father and the Son together undergo in the Incarnation, which in all Christian theology involves a kind of mingling of the two divine natures. Neither God nor Christ requires personality for Paul, who possessed so much of that quality that he scarcely needed to seek it outside of himself. Because the Resurrection was, for Paul, entirely spiritual (I Corinthians 15:44), personality becomes irrelevant. When Freud says that the ego is always a bodily ego, he would not provoke Paul. To Paul, Christ is the Son of God, and not the Son of Man, though Paul never says that Jesus declared he was the Messiah. Mark in this respect is consonant with Paul, unlike Matthew and John.

Paul transmits aspects of the Incarnation-Atonement complex, which he inherited from Hellenistic Christianity, presumably in Antioch and Damascus, where Diaspora Jewish Christians had been converting Gentiles. Scholars agree that we do not know where it was that the ideas of Incarnation and Atonement were first fused. Until the Gospel of John, the Incarnation is not central, perhaps because it depends upon the Pre-Existence of Christ, who comes down from heaven. Paul evades Incarnation in favor of Incorporation into the Spiritual Body of Christ Resurrected. In the Letter to the Philippians (2:6–11), Paul quotes a hymn, of undetermined origins, in which *kenosis* receives its earliest Christian emphasis:

> who, though he was in the form of God,
>
> did not count equality with God
>
> a thing to be grasped,
>
> but emptied himself,
>
> taking the form of a servant,
>
> being born in the likeness of men.
>
> And being found in human form
>
> he humbled himself
>
> and became obedient unto death,
>
> even death on a cross.
>
> Therefore God has highly exalted him
>
> and bestowed on him the name
>
> which is above every name,
>
> that at the name of Jesus
>
> every knee should bow,
>
> in heaven and on earth and under the earth,
>
> and every tongue confess
>
> that Jesus Christ is Lord,
>
> to the glory of God the Father.

The Parousia, or Second Coming of Christ, by then the fabled expectation of the first generation of Christians, edges everything that Paul writes. If Christ were to arrive again so soon, then Incorporation takes on particular urgency. Adam to Moses was *before* the Law; Moses to Christ was the realm of the Law; now the Coming End is all but upon Paul. It seems wrong to speak of Paul's theology, because the rapidly approaching conclusion renders theology unnecessary.

Paul is famously eloquent, though more in the English Bible than in the original. Yet he is an obsessed crank, who confuses anyone attempting a dispassionate stance toward him. And he is not truly an innovator or a reformer, but primarily a polemicist who defends a faith to which he has been converted. Neither a villain nor an exemplar, he is a singularly strange genius of synthesis who conceals something evasive in his deepest self. One shrugs off speculations as to his psychosexuality: why does that much matter? He distrusts mystical enthusiasm, perhaps because his crucial trust is in the Resurrection as an event in the Spirit yet also in outward history. Had he confronted the Valentinian Christian Gnosticism of a century later, he would have been outraged by the contention that *first* Jesus resurrected, and *then* he died. Something like that is what he combats in the Corinthians.

There is nothing Gentile about Paul, though he was the foremost apostle to them, as was confirmed by his agreement with James, the brother of Jesus. His ways of thinking and feeling essentially remained Pharisaic. Yahweh and Israel, Paul implies, will work out the Chosen People's Redemption. Did Paul, who must have died still expecting Christ's return, really believe that Israel would accept Christ at *that* moment? I have no answer, except that Paul's Messiah certainly has little in common with what the Jews expected, since they awaited a victorious warrior. But then his Christ also has not much in common with Yeshua of Nazareth, in any of his Gospel versions, even in John. Paul's delusion (what else could you call it?) is that he lives in the End Time. Myself a Gnostic Jew, I cannot pretend to understand Paul, almost two millennia later. Yet who can understand him? His best exegete, Wayne Meeks, tells us that "one may reasonably doubt whether an accurate and consistent judgment of the apostle is possible." We know too little about Yeshua of Nazareth to make any accurate statement whatsoever about him. We know too much about Paul, and I am left baffled by him. He could be a Shakespearean character, as enigmatic as Hamlet or Iago.

6.

THE GOSPEL OF MARK

THE GOSPELS, as we now possess them, evidently were composed from roughly thirty years to more than half a century after the Crucifixion of Yeshua. They concern themselves almost exclusively with the three final years of his life, perhaps between the ages of thirty-seven and forty. The Gospel of John, however, seems to deal mostly with his last ten weeks. Assuming that he was born about 6 B.C.E., that might date the Crucifixion at about 34 C.E., or seventeen years before Paul's first surviving epistle. Mark, almost certainly the earliest Gospel, generally is assigned to the time of the Jewish Revolt against Rome, 66–70 C.E., culminating in the devastation of the Temple.

We do not know who Mark was, or where he wrote, except that it was not in the Land of Israel. He is very unlikely to have known Yeshua, as were Matthew and Luke. Whether Mark, like the others, relied upon an earlier Christian writing, we cannot tell, yet I am always dubious about the pure transmission of oral traditions. What is certain is that none of the Gospels in itself represents a reliable account of what their Messiah taught, whether by word or act.

As literature, Mark's Gospel is considerably more impressive in the English Bible than in the Greek original, where an extraordinary sensibility struggles with inadequate language. Mark oddly fuses a kind of Yahwistic realism with an extremely abrupt narrative style, in which speed and immediacy are emphasized. Paula Fredriksen, in her *From Jesus to Christ* (1988, 2000), remarks that Mark's protagonist "is a man in a hurry." He is also a total enigma, given to asking his auditors (and Mark's readers): "Who do people say I am?" How open is that question? Does this version of Jesus have an initial insight as to his own precise identity, or does he achieve it only near the end?

Barry Qualls remarks on the affinity between Mark and the Yahwist, and Isaiah, all of whom divide up their potential audience into those who will understand and those who cannot confront divine riddling. It is not that Jesus, like J's Yahweh, is impish. Jesus is not playful, and yet at times he is willing to mystify. Yet both Gods (or aspects of God) are uncanny, unexpected though close to home. Mark's Jesus also will be present where and when he chooses.

If you haven't read straight through the Gospel of Mark (or not recently), a kind of shock is inevitable when you attempt it. Challenge is only one part of the encounter; others include bewilderment of our understanding, and a sense of the forlorn in regard to our expectations. Apocalypse hovers throughout: the final events are near. Whether the Jewish War is ongoing, or Jerusalem already has been destroyed, we are never told, but Mark lives in what he believes to be the end time. The weirdness of the entire New Testament is that everyone in it is utterly persuaded that Christ soon will return. Two thousand years later, he has not. So committed is the text to imminence that I murmur, while rereading, an old rabbinical adage: "Let the Messiah come, but may I not be there to see it." Mark's author, like his Jesus, is hurried yet secretive, and not particularly eager to assist us in interpreting the Good News. Like the disciples themselves, we see without discerning. Poor Peter, dreadfully confused, is rebuked by Jesus with customary authority, and is told that, however momentarily, disciple and Satan are become as one. Only the devils (and Mark) invariably know exactly what Jesus is.

Frank Kermode, in his *The Genesis of Secrecy* (1979), emphasized the peculiar paradoxical quality of Mark's narrative:

> But there are many knots; they occur in the riddling parables, in the frequent collocation of perceptive demons and imperceptive saints, in the delight and gratitude of the outsider who is cured, and the astonishment, fear, and dismay of the insiders. (p. 141)

Almost all New Testament scholars, and other believing Christians, think they are delighted and grateful insiders. Are they? Does their sainthood transcend that of the disciples? I hardly think we as yet have absorbed the discomfort that only what is demonic *in us* can accurately perceive the identity of Christ Jesus. Mark is both a bad writer and a great one: I think of Edgar Allan Poe as another rare instance of *that* paradox, insane as my juxtaposition must seem. Is the strange conclusion of Mark's Gospel a mark (as it were) of ineptitude or of genius? Truncation there makes us identify with the women at the tomb; we too flee because we are afraid:

When the sabbath was over, Mary Magdalene, and Mary the mother of James, and Salome bought spices, so that they might go and anoint him. And very early on the first day of the week, when the sun had risen, they went to the tomb. They had been saying to one another, "Who will roll away the stone for us from the entrance to the tomb?" When they looked up, they saw that the stone, which was very large, had already been rolled back. As they entered the tomb, they saw a young man, dressed in a white robe, sitting on the right side; and they were alarmed. But he said to them, "Do not be alarmed; you are looking for Jesus of Nazareth, who was crucified. He has been raised; he is not here. Look, there is the place they laid him. But go, tell his disciples and Peter that he is going ahead of you to Galilee; there you will see him, as he told you." So they went out and fled from the tomb, for terror and amazement had seized them; and they said nothing to anyone, for they were afraid.

MARK 16:1−8

There the original text of Mark concludes; 16:9–20 is a later addition and palpably an editorial afterthought, attempting to remedy this striking abruptness. A Gospel whose favorite word is "immediately" (some forty occurrences), and which is jagged throughout, ends properly with three silent and devoted women hurrying away from what is no longer the tomb of Jesus. The Gospels are intended to proclaim the Good News of Redemption. Mark ends with "for they were afraid," hardly a tonality of salvation. Kermode comments, "The conclusion is either intolerably clumsy, or it is incredibly subtle." A choice between the intolerable and the incredible is rather a charming one, and I suspect we need not choose: Mark, by turns, is both clumsy and subtle (again, like Poe). We all know such people, though usually they are not writers. But then, Mark is not primarily a writer. Probably a resident of Rome, he anxiously awaits and then receives the terrible news of the utter destruction of the Temple. In the shadow of Isaiah, he nevertheless aspires to be himself a prophet. He *proclaims* in a Hebraic tradition, and with considerable anxiety in regard to his prime precursor, the first Isaiah, surely the grandest of the prophets after Moses himself. Mark at once needs Isaiah and doesn't want him, because the prophet has to be superseded, by fulfillment in Christ. Since Mark's Jesus is secretive, as is Mark, it is difficult both to reveal and conceal a truth that transcends Isaiah's Yahwism. If Isaiah's auditors could be uncomprehending, then Mark swerves from Isaiah by portraying the disciples as not very bright students of a quicksilver master who brings "a new teaching!" (1:27). Perhaps Jesus is impatient, as would be any baffling teacher who tries to abrogate a strong prior mode that here is not less than Torah. The disciples, in Mark, cannot wholly be blamed. It is not until Chapter 13:14–27 that they are let into the secret:

> "But when you see the desolating sacrilege set up where it ought not
> to be (let the reader understand), then those in Judea must flee to the
> mountains; the one on the housetop must not go down or enter the
> house to take anything away; the one in the field must not turn back
> to get a coat. Woe to those who are pregnant and to those who are
> nursing infants in those days! Pray that it may not be in winter. For in
> those days there will be suffering, such as has not been from the be-
> ginning of the creation that God created until now, no, and never
> will be. And if the Lord had not cut short those days, no one would

be saved; but for the sake of the elect, whom he chose, he has cut short those days. And if anyone says to you at that time, 'Look! Here is the Messiah!' or 'Look, There he is!'—do not believe it. False messiahs and false prophets will appear and produce signs and omens, to lead astray, if possible, the elect. But be alert; I have already told you everything.

"But in those days, after that suffering,

the sun will be darkened,

and the moon will not give

its light,

and the stars will be falling

from heaven,

and the powers in the heavens

will be shaken.

Then they will see 'the Son of Man coming in clouds' with great power and glory. Then he will send out the angels, and gather his elect from the four winds, from the ends of the earth to the ends of heaven."

The abomination of desolation set up in the Temple is from Daniel 9:27 and, more crucially, so is Mark's version of the "Son of Man," which in the Aramaic text only means "one like a human being":

As I looked on, in the night vision,

One like a human being

Came with the clouds of heaven;

He reached the Ancient of Days

And was presented to Him.

Dominion, glory, and kingship were given to him;

All peoples and nations of every language must serve him.

His dominion is an everlasting dominion that shall not pass

    away,

And his kingship, one that shall not be destroyed.

DANIEL 7:13−14

Mark's persuasive misreading changes "one like a human being" into the apocalyptic term "Son of Man." That leads to the larger paradox of this cryptic Gospel. Since both Matthew and Luke derive from Mark, it is not too much to say that the Marcan highly individual and mysterious Jesus has become normative. Pragmatically, has Mark not invented the Jesus of faith? I do not mean literally invented, since followers of Jesus had been proclaiming him as the Son of God for at least a quarter century before Mark wrote. But they left us no texts, though I continue to be convinced that Mark followed written sources. Did such earlier works portray Mark's highly individual and mysterious Jesus? Enigmas, in my literary experience, do not transmit readily and tend to undergo considerable modification. Reflect that Matthew and Luke give us a Jesus considerably less capricious than Mark's. Indeed the Gospels of Matthew and Luke scarcely resemble Mark's wavering portrait of an ambivalent Jesus who makes himself immensely difficult to comprehend. Once John the Baptist vanishes from Mark's story, everything about Jesus becomes really ambiguous. He provokes astonishment in all he encounters, and the obsessive emphasis upon the shock he evokes is too idiosyncratic not to be Mark's own invention. Family, disciples, enemies, and the crowds of witnesses are overcome by the newness they confront.

The Marcan Jesus is a master of silences, which we are invited to understand, *if we can*. This is not the Christ preached by Paul, or the Son of God presented by Matthew and Luke, let alone the cosmic Christ of the Gospel of John. Whoever composed Mark is a genius still too original for us to absorb, though a weird Gospel might seem an oxymoron. Raymond E. Brown, a superb New Testament scholar, took a very different stance on this matter:

> Writing disparagingly of much biblical criticism, Kermode stresses Marcan obscurity, so that amid moments of radiance, basically the Gospel remains a mystery like the parables, arbitrarily excluding readers from the kingdom. Leaving aside the critiques of Kermode's book as to whether he has understood exegesis and has not substituted art for science, one may object that he has isolated Mark's writing from its ultimate Christian theology. The motifs of disobedience, failure, misunderstanding, and darkness are prominent in Mark; but the death of Jesus on the cross, which is the darkest moment in the Gospel, is not the end. God's power breaks through, and an outsider like the Roman centurion is not excluded but understands. No matter how puzzled the women at the tomb are, the readers are not left uncertain: Christ is risen and he can be seen. (*An Introduction to the New Testament*, 1997, pp. 153–54)

I would only reply to Brown that Mark's writing and "its ultimate Christian theology" are not necessarily identical. The centurion may understand, but the devoted women at the tomb do not, and without the later verses added by Christian editors, many readers would remain very uncertain. God's power breaks through only in the theological gloss appended as 16:9–20, which is not authored by Mark, whose Jesus cries out, in Aramaic, "My God, my God, why hast thou forsaken me?" (15:34) and then utters a loud, wordless cry and dies. The anguished lament echoes the opening of Psalm 22, and Mark's text does not elaborate the pain and despair in which Jesus dies.

MARK FOLLOWS ISAIAH closely in a passage I find extraordinarily memorable, and which I have already quoted. Here, once again, is Isaiah 6:8–10, followed by Mark 4:10–12.

> Then I heard the voice of my Lord saying, "Whom shall I send? Who will go for us?" And I said, "Here am I; send me." And He said, "Go, say to that people:
>   'Hear, indeed, but do not understand.
>   See, indeed, but do not grasp.'
>   Dull that people's mind,
>   Stop its ears,
>   And seal its eyes—
>   Lest, seeing with its eyes
>   And hearing with its ears,
>   It also grasp with its mind,
>   And repent and save itself."

When he was alone, those who were around him along with the twelve asked him about the parables. And he said to them, "To you has been given the secret of the kingdom of God, but for those outside, everything comes in parables; in order that 'they may indeed look, but not perceive,

and may indeed listen, but not understand;

so that they may not turn again and be forgiven.'"

Kermode, confronting the enigma of Mark's passage and its source in Isaiah, usefully juxtaposes Matthew's softening of Mark, in the Gospel of Matthew 13:10–17:

Then the disciples came and asked him, "Why do you speak to them in parables?" He answered, "To you it has been given to know the secrets of the kingdom of heaven, but to them it has not been given. For to those who have, more will be given, and they will have an abundance; but from those who have nothing, even what they have will be taken away. The reason I speak to them in parables is that 'seeing they do not perceive, and hearing they do not listen, nor do they understand.' With them indeed is fulfilled the prophecy of Isaiah that says:

'You will indeed listen, but never understand,

and you will indeed look, but never perceive.

For this people's heart has grown dull,

and their ears are hard of hearing,

and they have shut their eyes;

so that they might not look with their eyes,

and listen with their ears,

and understand with their heart and turn—

and I would heal them.'

But blessed are your eyes, for they see, and your ears, for they hear.

> Truly, I tell you, many prophets and righteous people longed
> to see what you see, but did not see it, and to hear what you hear,
> but did not hear it.

The Parable of the Sower, which appears both in Mark and Matthew, represents the attempt by Jesus to sow the Word of God, and in Mark the disciples hopelessly fail to understand. Birds devouring the Savior's seeds belong to, indeed are, Satan. Does Mark understand either the parable or Jesus' interpretation? Though Mark doesn't say so, we have to assume that he knew that his Jesus was alluding to Isaiah's bitter irony, in which Yahweh sends forth a willing prophet while remarking that he will not be understood. Matthew, softening Mark's harshness, overtly quotes Isaiah, thus giving us a rather more conventional Jesus, who can shrug off any slowness of understanding, whether among the people or his own disciples. But what happens to Mark's utterly characteristic sense of how mysterious Jesus is, if we accept Matthew's revision?

Barry Qualls, following Kermode, illuminates Mark for me more strongly than critics I have encountered elsewhere. Here is Qualls, in his essay "Saint Mark Says They Mustn't" (*Raritan* VIII:4 [Spring 1989]):

> The New Testament authors provide in their self-consciousness the final examples of this confrontation at work *and* of the anxieties it produced among writers determined to form a faith that would triumph over the contingencies of history. Only Mark, willing to take "captive" the Hebrew texts, is also at ease with their gaps and resulting ambiguities—and with the work of reading and interpreting those gaps demand.

. . .

[H]ow unlike the Christian writers who came after him Mark is, and how much he is like the early Hebrew writers, especially the Yahwist. Mark is the Gospel writer who most strongly comprehends, and does not fear, the Yahwist's willingness to entertain the contradictory and the ambiguous, the Hebrew determination to summon the reader to take part in the story. Mark is sublimely at ease with the gaps. "(Let him that readeth understand)," he says in an astonishing parenthesis inserted into the chapter (13:14) where he writes his own apocalypse (with echoes of Daniel). Understanding or, rather, the difficulty of understanding is indeed his theme, as it is the theme of the Hebrew writers who, sure in God's words, must still record how distant those promises seem from the actions and difficulties of human beings. In Mark we glimpse for one last time in the (Christian) Bible the freedom of the Yahwist encountering and recounting, without awe or fear, the acts of his God. After Mark, the text *is* taken into captivity. But Mark, obsessed with "mysteriousness, silence, and incomprehension," as Kermode says, "prefers the shadows." He prefers to let readers, like his disciples, see, hear, possibly understand, and almost certainly deny.

. . .

His strategies of characterization show an author striving for ambiguity. His "Son of God" is always in crowds and always seeking an isolated place, always speaking and yet urging silence, always explaining and yet certain his words will not be understood. His family, who enter the text without introduction, are amazed by his denial of them (3:31–35); his friends are certain "he is beside himself" (3:21); and his enemies, not surprisingly, echo these responses and add others. The disciples question "what manner of man is this" from early on (4:41) and are repeatedly "astonished at his words," questioning what such use of language signifies. (Their idea of kingship involves which of them will "be greatest" in an earthly kingdom; it seems incomprehensible that a kingdom might be compared to a mustard seed, parable or not.) Even Mark's own asserted phrase, "Son of God," is repeated in such a way as to undercut its authority. Its only appearances in the text after the opening are in the mouths of the demon-possessed, who have no trouble seeing Jesus' connection with God (see 5:7), and at the end, in the words of the Roman centurion as he hears Jesus cry from the cross: "Truly this man was the Son of God" (15:39). Otherwise, we hear others call him the "son of David." We hear him often name himself the "Son of man." And we hear Peter say, "Thou art the Christ," and then show so little understanding of what he means by the words that Jesus says to him, "Get thee behind me, Satan" (8:29, 33). No wonder we feel so much "astonishment" when the captive Jesus replies to the high priest's question, "Art thou the Christ?": "I am" (14:62).

What Qualls captures is the shocking immediacy of Mark's stance, his renewal of the J Writer's freedom in representing Yahweh as an exalted but all-too-human man. When I argue, throughout this book, that the theological God, the Jesus-the-Christ of the Gospel of John and subsequent Catholic theology, is clearly irreconcilable with Yahweh, I partly mean that Trinitarian Jesus Christ is Greek and Yahweh is precisely what forever resists Greek thought in Hebrew tradition. But two versions of Jesus, Mark's and aspects of the person revealed in the quasi-Gnostic Gospel of Thomas, are profoundly compatible with

J's Yahweh. It is a puzzle to me that the Jesus in Mark and the Jesus in the Gospel of Thomas have little to nothing in common with each other, but the wildly capacious, original Yahweh had room enough for both.

Mark takes a gloomy pride in the disturbing newness of his Jesus, but then J's Yahweh is forever disconcerting also. Both man-gods (a desperate phrase, but what alternative?) break down the limits that supposedly define the border between the anthropomorphic and the theomorphic. The Jesus of Mark is secretive, while J's Yahweh is child-like and bold, yet Qualls is clearly justified in linking this Jesus to the Yahweh who is always master of the unexpected. I myself, speaking now only as a literary critic, am not persuaded that the Jesus of Matthew or of Luke is truly the Son of God. Yet, again only as a critic, I would grant Mark his curious literary power, Poe-like in its grotesqueness, that indeed suggests a Son of Yahweh is alive in his pages.

7.

THE GOSPEL OF JOHN

Your father Abraham rejoiced that he was to see my day; he saw it and was glad.' The Jews then said to him, 'You are not yet fifty years old, and have you seen Abraham?' Jesus said to them, 'Truly, truly, I say to you, before Abraham was, I am'" (John 8:56–58).

It is now altogether too late in Western history for pious or humane self-deceptions on the matter of the Christian appropriation of the Hebrew Bible. It is certainly much too late in Jewish history to be other than totally clear about the nature and effect of that Christian act of total usurpation. The best preliminary description I have found is by Jaroslav Pelikan:

> What the Christian tradition had done was to take over the Jewish Scriptures as its own, so that Justin could say to Trypho that the passages about Christ "are contained in your Scriptures, or rather not yours, but ours." As a matter of fact, some of the passages were con-

tained only in "ours," that is, in the Christian Old Testament. So assured were Christian theologians in their possession of the Scriptures that they could accuse the Jews not merely of misunderstanding and misinterpreting them, but even of falsifying scriptural texts. When they were aware of differences between the Hebrew text of the Old Testament and the Septuagint, they capitalized on these to prove their accusation.... The growing ease with which appropriations and accusations alike could be made was in proportion to the completeness of the Christian victory over Jewish thought. Yet that victory was achieved largely by default. Not the superior force of Christian exegesis or learning or logic but the movement of Jewish history seems to have been largely responsible for it.

I come back again to the grand proclamation of John's Jesus: "Before Abraham was, I am." How should the sublime force of that assertion be described? Is it not the New Testament's antithetical reply to the Yahwist's most sublime moment, when Moses agonizingly stammers, "If I come to the people of Israel and say to them, 'The God of your fathers has sent me to you,' and they ask me, 'What is his name?' what shall I say to them?" God said to Moses, "I AM WHO I AM."

The Yahwist's vision of his God certainly would seem to center with a peculiar intensity upon this text of Exodus 3:13–14. But the entire history of ancient Jewish exegesis hardly would lead anyone to believe that this crucial passage was of the slightest interest or importance to any of the great rabbinical commentators. The *Exodus Rabbah* offers mostly midrashim connecting the name of God to his potencies that would deliver Israel from Egypt. But *ehyeh asher ehyeh* as a phrase evidently did not have peculiar force for the great Pharisees.

Indeed, Jewish tradition does very little with the majestic proclamation until, in the twelfth century, Maimonides gets to work upon it in *The Guide for the Perplexed*. One of my favorite books, Arthur Marmorstein's fascinating *The Old Rabbinic Doctrine of God*, has absolutely not a single reference to Exodus 3 in its exhaustive 150-page section "The Names of God." Either we must conclude that *ehyeh asher ehyeh* had very little significance for Akiba and his colleagues, which I think probably was the case, or we must resort to dubious theories of taboo, which have little to do with the strength of Akiba.

This puzzle becomes greater when the early rabbinical indifference to the striking *ehyeh asher ehyeh* text is contrasted with the Christian obsession with Exodus 3, which begins in the New Testament and becomes overwhelming in the Church Fathers, culminating in Augustine's endless preoccupation with that passage, since for Augustine it was the deepest clue to the metaphysical essence of God. Brevard Childs, in his commentary on Exodus, has outlined the history of this long episode in Christian exegesis. Respectfully, I dissent from his judgment that the ontological aspects of Christian interpretation here really do have any continuity whatsoever either with the biblical text or with rabbinical traditions. These "ontological overtones," as Childs himself has to note, stem rather from the Septuagint's rendering and from Philo's very Platonized paraphrase in his *On the Life of Moses*: "Tell them that I am He Who is, that they may learn the difference between what is and what is not." Though Childs insists that this cannot be dismissed as Greek thinking, it is nothing but that, and explains again why Philo was so crucial for Christian theology and so totally irrelevant to the continuity of normative Judaism.

The continued puzzle, then, is the total lack of early rabbinical interest in the *ehyeh asher ehyeh* text. I labor this point because I read John's greatest subversion of the Hebrew Bible as what I call his transformation of Yahweh's words to Moses in the extraordinary outburst of John's Jesus, "Before Abraham was, I am," which most deeply proclaims, "Before Moses was, I am." To me, this is the acutest manifestation of John's palpable ambivalence toward Moses, an ambivalence whose most perceptive student has been Wayne Meeks. John plays on and against the Yahwist's grand wordplay on Yahweh and *ehyeh*. However, when I assert even that, I go against the authority of the leading current scholarly commentary upon the Fourth Gospel, and so I must deal with this difficulty before I return to the Johannine ambivalence toward the Moses traditions. And only after examining John's agon with Moses will I feel free to speculate upon the early rabbinic indifference to God's substitution of *ehyeh asher ehyeh* for his proper name.

Both B. Lindars and C. K. Barrett, in their standard commentaries on John, insist that "Before Abraham was, I am" makes no allusion whatsoever to "I am that I am." A literary critic must begin by observing that New Testament scholarship manifests a very impoverished notion as to just what literary allusion is or can be, even in so extraordinary a figuration. But then here is Barrett's flat reading of this assertion of Jesus: "The meaning here is: Before Abraham came into being, I eternally was, as now I am, and ever continue to be." The master modern interpreter of John, Rudolf Bultmann, seems to me even less capable of handling metaphor. Here is his reading of John 8:57–58:

The Jews remain caught in the trammels of their own thought. How can Jesus, who is not yet 50 years old, have seen Abraham! *Yet* the world's conception of time and age is worthless, when it has to deal with God's revelation, as is its conception of life and death. "Before Abraham was, I am." The Revealer, unlike Abraham, does not belong to the ranks of historical personages. The *ego* which Jesus speaks as the Revealer is the "I" of the eternal Logos, which was in the beginning, the "I" of the eternal God himself. Yet the Jews cannot comprehend that the ego of eternity is to be heard in an historical person, who is not yet 50 years old, who as a man is one of their equals, whose mother and father they knew. They cannot understand, because the notion of the Revealer's "pre-existence" can only be understood in faith.

In a note, Bultmann too denies any allusion to the "I am that I am" declaration of Yahweh. I find it ironical, nearly two thousand years after St. Paul accused the Jews of being literalizers, that the leading scholars of Christianity are hopeless literalizers, which of course the great rabbis never were. I cannot conceive of a weaker misreading of "Before Abraham was, I am" than Bultmann's retreat into "faith," a "faith" in the "pre-existence" of Jesus. While I—or anyone—cannot question an argument based solely upon faith, if that is all John meant, then John was a weak poet indeed. But John is at his best here, and at his best he is a strong misreader and thus a strong writer. As for Bultmann's polemical point, I am content to repeat a few remarks made by Rabbi David Kimhi almost eight hundred years ago:

Tell them that there can be no father and son in the Divinity, for the Divinity is indivisible and is one in every aspect of unity unlike matter which is divisible.

Tell them further that a father precedes a son in time and a son is born through the agency of a father. Now even though each of the terms "father" and "son" implies the other . . . he who is called the father must undoubtedly be prior in time. Therefore, with reference to this God whom you call Father, Son and Holy Spirit, that part which you call Father must be prior to that which you call Son, for if they were always coexistent, they would have to be called twin brothers.

I have cited this partly because I enjoy it so much, but also because it raises the true issue between Moses and John, between Abraham and Jesus, which is the agonistic triple issue of priority, authority, and originality. As I read John's trope, it asserts not only the priority of Jesus over Abraham (and so necessarily over Moses), but also the priority, authority, and originality of John over Moses, or as we would say, of John as writer over the Yahwist as writer. That is where I am heading in this account of the agon between the Yahwist and John, and so I turn now to some general observations upon the Fourth Gospel— observations by a literary critic, of course, and not by a qualified New Testament believer and/or scholar.

John does seem to me the most anxious in tone of all the Gospels, and its anxiety is as much what I would call a literary anxiety as an existential or spiritual one. One sign of this anxiety is the palpable difference between the attitude of Jesus toward himself in the Fourth Gospel as compared with the other three. Scholarly consensus holds that John was written at the close of the first century, and so after the Synoptic Gospels. A century is certainly enough time for apocalyptic hope to have ebbed away, and for an acute sense of belatedness to have developed in its place. John's Jesus has a certain obsession with his own glory, and particularly with what that glory ought to be in a Jewish context. Rather like the Jesus of Gnosticism, John's Jesus is much given to saying "I am," and there are Gnostic touches throughout John, though their extent is disputable. Perhaps, as some scholars have surmised, there is an earlier, more Gnostic gospel buried in the Gospel of John. An interesting article by John Meagher of Toronto, back in 1969, even suggested that the original reading of John 1:14 was "And the Word became *pneuma* and dwelt among us," which is a Gnostic formulation, yet curiously more in the spirit and tone of much of the Fourth Gospel than is "And the Word became flesh."

The plain nastiness of the Gospel of John toward the Pharisees is in the end an anxiety as to the spiritual authority of the Pharisees, and it may be augmented by John's Gnostic overtones. A Jewish reader with even the slightest sense of Jewish history feels threatened when reading John 18:28–19:16. I do not think that this feeling has anything to do with the supposed pathos or problematic literary power of the text. There is a peculiar wrongness about John's Jesus saying, "If my kingship were of this world, my servants would fight, that I might not be handed over to the Jews" (18:36); it implies that Jesus is no longer a Jew, but something else. This unhappy touch is another sign of the pervasive rhetoric of anxiety in the Fourth Gospel. John's vision seems to be of a small group—his own, presumably—which finds its analogue and asserted origin in the group around Jesus two generations before. In the general judgment of scholars, the original conclusion of the Gospel of John was the parable of doubting Thomas, a manifest metaphor for a sect or coven undergoing a crisis of faith.

It is within that anxiety of frustrated expectations, perhaps even of recent expulsion from the Jewish world, that John's agon with Moses finds its context. Wayne Meeks has written very sensitively of the Fourth Gospel's ambivalence toward the Moses traditions, particularly those centered upon the image of Moses as prophet-king, a unique amalgam of the two roles that John seeks to extend and surpass in Jesus. John, and Paul before him, took on an impossible precursor and rival, and their apparent victory is merely an illusion. The aesthetic dignity of the Hebrew Bible, and of the Yahwist in particular as its uncanny original, is simply beyond the competitive range of the New Testament as a literary achievement, as it is beyond the range of the only surviving Gnostic texts that have any aesthetic value—a few fragments of Valentinus and the Gospel of Truth, which Valentinus may have written.

There are so many contests with Moses throughout the New Testament that I cannot contrast John in this regard with all the other references, but I do want to compare him briefly with Paul, if only because I intend later to consider some aspects of Paul's own struggle with the Hebrew Bible. I think there is still nothing so pungent in all commentary upon Paul as the remarks made by Nietzsche in 1888, in *The Antichrist*:

> Paul is the incarnation of a type which is the reverse of that of the Savior; he is the genius in hatred, in the standpoint of hatred, and in the relentless logic of hatred. . . . What he wanted was power; with St. Paul the priest again aspired to power,—he could make use only of concepts, doctrines, symbols with which masses may be tyrannised over, and with which herds are formed.

Of course, Nietzsche is extreme, but can he be refuted? Paul is so careless, hasty, and inattentive a reader of the Hebrew Bible that he very rarely gets any text right; and in so gifted a person this kind of weak misunderstanding can come only from the dialectics of the power drive, of the will to power over a text, even when the text is as formidable as the Torah. There is little agonistic cunning in Paul's misreadings of the Torah; many indeed are plain howlers. The most celebrated is his weird exegesis of Exodus 34:29–35, where the text has Moses descending from Sinai, tablets in hand, his face shining with God's glory—a glory so great that Moses must veil his countenance after speaking to the people, and then unveil only when he returns to speak to God. Jewish interpretation, surely known to Paul, was that the shining was the Torah's restoration of the *zelem,* the true image of God that Adam had lost, and that the shining prevailed until the death of Moses. But here is II Corinthians 3:12–13:

> Since we have such a hope, we are very bold, not like Moses, who put
> a veil over his face so that the Israelites might not see the end of the
> fading splendor.

There isn't any way to save this, even by gently calling it a "parody" of the Hebrew text, as Wayne Meeks does. It isn't a lie against time, which is the Johannine mode; it is just a plain lie against the text. Nor is it uncharacteristic of Paul. Meeks very movingly calls Paul "the Christian Proteus," and Paul is certainly beyond my understanding. Proteus is an apt model for many other roles, but perhaps not for an interpreter of Mosaic text. Paul's reading of what he thought was the Law increasingly seems to me oddly Freudian, in that Paul identifies the Law with the human drive that Freud wanted to call Thanatos. Paul's peculiar confounding of the Law and death presumably keeps him from seeing Jesus as a transcending fulfillment of Moses. Instead, Paul contrasts himself with Moses, hardly to his own disadvantage. Thus, Romans 9:3:

> For I could wish that I myself were accused and cut off from Christ
> for the sake of my brethren, my kinsmen by race.

Paul's outburst may seem at first one of Jewish pride, of which I would grant the Protean Paul an authentic share, but the Mosaic allusion changes its nature. All exegetes point to Exodus 32:32 as the precursor text. Moses offers himself to Yahweh as atonement for the people after the orgy of the Golden Calf: "But now, if thou wilt forgive their sin—and if not, blot me, I pray thee, out of thy book which thou hast written." How do the two offers of intercession compare? After all, the people *have* sinned, and Moses would choose oblivion to save them from the consequences of their disloyalty. The allusive force of Paul's offer is turned against both his own Jewish contemporaries and even against Moses himself. Even the Pharisees (for whom Paul, unlike John, has a lingering regard) are worshipers of the golden calf of death, since the Law *is* death. And all Moses supposedly offered was the loss of his own prophetic greatness, his place in the salvation history. But Paul, out of supposed love for his fellow Jews, offers to lose more than Moses did, because he insists he has more to lose. To be cut off from Christ is to die eternally, a greater sacrifice than the

Mosaic offer to be as one who had never lived. This is what I would call the daemonic counter-Sublime of hyperbole, and its repressive force is enormous and very revelatory.

But I return again to John, whose revisionary warfare against Moses is subtler. Meeks has traced the general pattern, and so I follow him here, though of course he would dissent from the interpretation I am going to offer of this pattern of allusion. The allusions begin with John the Baptist chanting a typical Johannine reversal, in which the latecomer truly has priority ("John bore witness to him, and cried, 'This was he of whom I said: He who comes after me ranks before me, for he was before me'"), to which the author of the Fourth Gospel adds, "For the law was given through Moses; grace and truth came through Jesus Christ" (John 1:15, 17). Later, the first chapter proclaims, "We have found him of whom Moses in the law and also the prophets wrote, Jesus of Nazareth" (1:45). The third chapter daringly inverts a great Mosaic trope in a way still unnerving for any Jewish reader: "No one has ascended into heaven but he who descended from heaven, the Son of man. And as Moses lifted up the serpent in the wilderness, so must the Son of man be lifted up" (3:13–14). John's undoubted revisionary genius is very impressive here merely from a technical or rhetorical point of view. No heavenly revelations ever were made to Moses. Jesus on the cross will be the antithetical completion of the Mosaic raising of the brazen serpent in the wilderness. Moses was only a part, but Jesus is the fulfilling whole. My avoidance of the language of typology, here and elsewhere, is deliberate.

The same ratio of antithetical completion is invoked when Jesus announces himself as the fulfiller of the sign of manna, as would be expected of the Messiah. But here the gratuitous ambivalence toward

Moses is sharper: "Truly, truly, I say to you, it was not Moses who gave you the bread from heaven; my father gives you the true bread from heaven. For the bread of God is that which comes down from heaven, and gives life to the world" (6:32–33). As the metaphor is developed, it becomes deliberately so shocking in a Jewish context that even the disciples are startled; but I would point to one moment in the development as marking John's increasing violence against Moses and all the Jews: "Your fathers ate the manna in the wilderness, and they died. . . . I am the living bread . . . if any one eats of this bread, he will live for ever; and the bread which I shall give for the life of the world is my flesh" (6:49, 51). It is, after all, gratuitous to say that our fathers ate the manna and died; it is even misleading, since had they not eaten the manna, they would not have lived as long as they did. But John has modulated to a daemonic counter-Sublime, and his hyperbole helps to establish a new, Christian sublimity, in which Jews die and Christians live eternally.

Rather than multiply instances of John's revisionism, I want to conclude my specific remarks on the Fourth Gospel by examining in its full context the passage with which I began: "Before Abraham was, I am." I am more than a little unhappy with the sequence I will expound, because I find in it John at nearly his most unpleasant and indeed anti-Jewish, but the remarkable rhetorical strength of "Before Abraham was, I am" largely depends upon its contextualization, as John undoes the Jewish pride in being descended from Abraham. The sequence, extending through most of the eighth chapter, begins with Jesus sitting in the Temple, surrounded both by Pharisees and by Jews who are in the process of becoming his believers. To those he has begun to persuade, Jesus now says what is certain to turn them away:

"If you continue in my word, you are truly my disciples, and you will know the truth, and the truth will make you free." They answered him, "We are descendants of Abraham, and have never been in bondage to anyone. How is it that you say, 'You will be made free'?"

8:31–33

It seems rather rhetorically weak that Jesus should then become aggressive, with a leap into murderous insinuations:

"I know that you are descendants of Abraham; yet you seek to kill me, because my word finds no place in you. I speak of what I have seen with my Father, and you do what you have heard from your father."

8:37–38

As John's Jesus graciously is about to tell them, the Jews' father is the devil. They scarcely can be blamed for answering, "Abraham is our father," or for assuming that their accuser has a demon. I look at the foot of the page of the text I am using, *The New Oxford Annotated Bible, Revised Standard Version* (1977), and next to verse 48, on having a demon, the editors helpfully tell me, "*The Jews* turn to insult and calumny" (page 1300). I reflect upon how wonderful a discipline such scholarship is, and I mildly rejoin that by any dispassionate reading, John's Jesus has made the initial "turn to insult and calumny." What matter, since the Jews are falling neatly into John's rhetorical trap? Jesus has promised that his believers "will never see death," and the astonished children of Abraham (or children of the devil?) protest:

"Abraham died, as did the prophets; and you say, 'If any one keeps my word, he will never taste death.' Are you greater than our father Abraham, who died?"

8:52−53

Jesus responds by calling them liars, again surely rather gratuitously, and then by ensnaring them in John's subtlest entrapment, which will bring me full circle to where I began:

"Your father Abraham rejoiced that he was to see my day; he saw it and was glad." The Jews then said to him, "You are not yet fifty years old, and have you seen Abraham?" Jesus said to them, "Truly, truly, I say to you, before Abraham was, I am."

8:56−58

When John's Jesus says, "Before Abraham was, I am," the ultimate allusion is not to Abraham but to Moses, and to Yahweh's declaration made to Moses, "I am that I am." The metaphor leaps over Abraham by saying also, "Before Moses was, I am," and by hinting ultimately, "I am that I am"—because I am one with my father Yahweh. The ambivalence and agonistic intensity of the Fourth Gospel achieve an apotheosis with this sublime introjection of Yahweh, which simultaneously also is a projection or repudiation of Abraham and Moses.

Earlier in this discourse, I confessed my surprise at the normative rabbinical indifference, in ancient days, to Yahweh's sublime declaration *ehyeh asher ehyeh*. If the great Rabbi Akiba ever speculated about that enigmatic phrase, he kept it to himself. I doubt that he made any such speculations, because I do not think that fearless sage was in the habit of hoarding them, and I am not enough of a Kabbalist to think that Akiba harbored forbidden or esoteric knowledge. To the normative mind of the Judaism roughly contemporary with Jesus, there was evidently nothing remarkable in Yahweh's declining to give his name, and instead almost playfully asserting, 'Tell them that I who will be when and where I will be am the one who has sent you." That is how Yahweh talked, and how he was. But to the belated auditor of the Fourth Gospel, as to all our belated selves, "I am that I am" was and is a kind of *mysterium tremendum,* to use Rudolf Otto's language from his great book *The Idea of the Holy.* That mystery John sought to transcend with the formulation "Before Abraham was, I am." Prior to the text of Exodus was the text that John was writing, in which the Jews were to be swept away into the universe of death, while Jesus led John on to the universe of life.

I don't see how any authentic literary critic could judge John as anything better than a very flawed revisionist of the Yahwist, and Paul as something less than that, despite the peculiar pathos of his Protean personality. In the aesthetic warfare between the Hebrew Bible and the New Testament, there is just no contest, and if you think otherwise, then bless you.

But surely the issue is not aesthetic, I will be reminded. Well, we are all trapped in history, and the historical triumph of Christianity is fact. I am not moved to say anything about it. But I am moved to reject the idealized modes of interpretation that triumph has stimulated, from early typology on to the revival of *figura* by Erich Auerbach and the Blakean Great Code of Northrop Frye. No text, secular or religious, fulfills another text, and all who insist otherwise merely homogenize literature. As for the relevance of the aesthetic to the issue of the conflict between sacred texts, I doubt finally that much else is relevant to a strong reader who is not dominated by extraliterary persuasions or convictions. Reading *The Book of Mormon,* for instance, is a difficult aesthetic experience, and I would grant that not much in the New Testament subjects me to rigors of quite that range. But then John and Paul do not ask to be read against *The Book of Mormon.*

Can the New Testament be read as less polemically and destructively revisionary of the Hebrew Bible than it actually is? Not by me, anyway. But don't be too quick to shrug off a reading informed by an awareness of the ways of the antithetical, of the revisionary strategies devised by those latecomers who seek strength, and who will sacrifice truth to get strength even as they proclaim the incarnation of the truth beyond death. Nietzsche is hardly the favorite sage of contemporary New Testament scholars, but perhaps he still has something vital to teach them.

What do Jews and Christians gain by refusing to see that the revisionary desperation of the New Testament has made it permanently impossible to identify the Hebrew Bible with the Christian Old Testament? Doubtless there are social and political benefits in idealizations of "dialogue," but there is nothing more. It is not a contribution to the life of the spirit or the intellect to tell lies to one another or to oneself in order to bring about more affection or cooperation between Christians and Jews. Paul is hopelessly equivocal on nearly every subject, but to my reading he is clearly not a Jewish anti-Semite; yet his misrepresentation of Torah is absolute. John is evidently a Jewish anti-Semite, and the Fourth Gospel is pragmatically murderous as an anti-Jewish text. Yet it is theologically and emotionally central to Christianity. I give the last word to the Sage called Radak in Jewish tradition, the same David Kimhi whom I cited earlier. He quotes as proof-text Ezekiel 16:53: "I will turn their captivity, the captivity of Sodom and her daughters." And then Radak comments, rightly dismissing from his perspective all Christians as mere heretics from Judaism, "This verse is a reply to the Christian heretics who say that the future consolations have already been fulfilled. *Sodom is still overturned as it was and is still unsettled.*"

8.

JESUS AND CHRIST

D ID JESUS CONSIDER himself Christ, that is, "the anointed one," or Davidic Messiah? Unless you value the Gospel of John over the Synoptic Gospels, you are puzzled as to the answer. John is nonstop on this matter, but can be distrusted, partly because of his anti-Jewish over-and-under song, which may testify to his group's expulsion by the Judaic community. In the Synoptics, Jesus is evasive or secretive in regard to his identity, as we ought to expect, partly because of dangerous situations but clearly also from a considerable ambivalence in his own self-awareness. There is no reason to doubt that he and his followers knew of his Davidic descent, and the execution of John the Baptist was a shadow, if only because he and Jesus were kinsmen, by some accounts, quite aside from the Baptist's role as his mentor.

Yet how would Jesus have named himself, besides his rather ambiguous uses of "Son of God" and "Son of Man," both of them metaphorical? Hamlet saw himself as Death's ambassador to us, in an ironic parody of Jesus' role as divine envoy, something more than a prophet yet other than a messianic king. Jesus did not, like Muhammad, see himself as the seal of the prophets, and preferred to delay any precise definition of his calling, though always expressing certainty that Yahweh had called him. It is unclear whether he foretells catastrophe, though scholars tend to that view.

When Jesus names himself God's son, he does not appear to invite literalization. He probably would have regarded Joseph of Egypt and David, both Yahweh's favorites, as being also "Sons of God." All Israel, as children of Abraham, were Sons and Daughters of God, as Jesus surely said (despite the Gospel of John's insistence that Jesus called his fellow Jews the children of the devil). Only three times does Jesus claim God as his father in Mark, as opposed to thirty-one such assertions in Matthew, and well beyond one hundred in John. And no one quite agrees as to what precisely Jesus intended to mean by referring to himself as Son of Man. He was probably using the Aramaic emphasis in which Son of Man sharpened the precariousness of mortal men, which seems to be the import of the phrase in Daniel 7:13. There is very little basis in the Synoptics for the runaway Christianity of John and of theological tradition after him. Elliptical, ironic parabolist as Jesus was, it may well be that he was an enigma even to himself.

The central irony, for anyone who is not a Christian believer, is that the living Jesus of the Synoptics does *not* believe he is the Incarnation of Yahweh, and least of all at the moment of his death, when he despairingly asks his *abba* why he has been abandoned. Death and stories of resurrection make Jesus a Name Divine from prior to St. Paul onward, and necessarily the transition from Yeshua of Nazareth to Jesus Christ was performed by those who first accepted the Apostle

Paul's conversion. The Christian historical scholars who *most* persuade me—Father John Meier and E. P. Sanders—are not ironists and they differ on their receptivity to the supernatural, accepted by Meier on grounds of Catholic faith but largely avoided by Sanders, whose Jesus remains firmly Jewish, though as so autonomous a charismatic that he constitutes his own authority, transcending Tanakh. Sanders gives us a Jesus who had an unmediated relationship with Yahweh— perhaps not unique, since prophets on to John the Baptist possessed the same attribute.

The New Testament founds itself upon the sacred violence of the Crucifixion and its supposed aftermath, in which death by torture transmogrifies into rising from the dead. That is a very different mode from the uncanny turbulence of Yahweh, who cuts Covenants with his people yet is perfectly free to break out against them, and warns Moses upon Sinai that the elders privileged to picnic with him are not to approach too closely. Realistically, Yahweh shows awareness of his own King Lear–like temperament, much given to sudden furies. Lear's tragic flaw is that he demands too much love, silently and shrewdly derived by Shakespeare from the Yahweh of the Geneva Bible. There are several versions of Jesus Christ in the Greek New Testament, but even the Jesus of Mark, the most Yahwistic of the Gospels, is not prone to breaking out against us.

The center of the crossing from Jesus of Nazareth to Jesus Christ is a constellation we can name Incarnation → Crucified Messiah → Atonement, which is non-Judaic and yet clearly develops from the ferment of Second Temple sectarianism. From about the middle of the first century of the Common Era—say, two decades before the Roman destruction of the Temple in 70 C.E.—ideas of Incarnation

and Atonement were being worked out by a number of unnamed followers of Jesus, perhaps more in Syria than in the land of Israel, since
James the Just and his Jerusalem and Galilean followers essentially
were Christian Jews rather than Jewish Christians. Saul of Tarsus presumably became Paul the Apostle at Damascus or Antioch, and there-
after addressed his mission to the Gentiles, eventually by an uneasy
agreement with James the brother of Jesus, who had no interest in
converting them. The Incarnation distinctly is *not* a Pauline belief: a
Yahweh who commits suicide made no sense to Paul, who had been a
Pharisee-of-the-Pharisees. But since Paul's letters are our earliest extant Christian texts, the entire Incarnation-Atonement complex long
has been misidentified as his.

Akenson, in his *Surpassing Wonder,* traces all the components of
Incarnation-Atonement to a medley of Second Temple–era sources.
The Tanakh knows of no Son of God, but something like it hovers in
the "Aramaic Apocalypse" of Qumran (cave four). Son of Man, greatly
altered from the Book of Daniel, pervades the Book of Enoch, and the
shocking 4 Maccabees gives instances of national atonement by voluntary martyrdoms. None of this is canonically biblical, and all of it is
alien to what developed in normative Rabbinical Judaism. The Hebrew
Sages were outraged by the flamboyance of later evolutions in Christian doctrine, as four gods emerged into a new pantheon: Jesus Christ,
God the Father, and the wholly original Blessed Virgin Mother and
non-Judaic Holy Ghost, who shows little relation to the spirit of Yahweh that moved creatively over the face of the waters.

My prime subject in this book is not the movement from Jesus to
Christ, but the startling juxtaposition of two very different Divine

Names, Jesus Christ and Yahweh. And yet the gap between these two versions of God cannot be apprehended without some sense of the profound abyss between the historical Yeshua and the theological God, Jesus Christ. It is likely that Yeshua of Nazareth, had he somehow survived the Crucifixion and lived on into old age, would have regarded Christianity with amazement.

That is hardly an original observation on my part, and is unacceptable to many millions of Americans, however bewilderingly multiform their visions of Jesus have become. A surprising number of them think they already live in the Kingdom of Jesus, and yet he did not suggest that he himself was the Kingdom; so far as I can tell, he meant the reign of Yahweh alone, here and now, rather than in another world or in the far-off future.

What did "Kingdom" mean to Jesus? E. P. Sanders is clearest on this, in *Jesus and Judaism* (1985):

The nature of the sayings material will not allow us to be certain about the precise nuance which Jesus wished to give such a large concept as 'the kingdom of God.' We can see that 'kingdom' has a range of meanings in the synoptics, but we cannot see just how much emphasis should be placed on each meaning. We never have absolute certainty of authenticity, and we probably have the original context of any given saying seldom, if ever. Facts allow us to be fairly sure that Jesus looked for a future kingdom. But to some degree conclusions about nuance and emphasis still rest on analysis of sayings, and since this analysis will always be tentative, some things about Jesus' view of the kingdom can never be known with certainty.

Sanders tells us we cannot know precisely what Jesus expected. Can one suggest that Jesus also did not know? He did not commit what to him would have been blasphemy: usurpation of Yahweh's Kingdom, a concept that Christian theologians are still unable to clarify. Others have usurped, in his name, and doubtless will go on usurping. I can find no transgression of the Torah on the part of Jesus, though he properly employs Torah against Torah, particularly on divorce, toward which he demonstrated a kind of horror. Whether that reflected his familial situation, again one cannot know. Sanders absolves Jesus of blasphemy by observing that speaking *for* God was not at all forbidden. Prophets could be mistaken, but their misinterpretations were set aside, without violence.

The immediate followers of Jesus certainly expected the Kingdom to come in their own lifetimes. Paul, belated Apostle, must have gone to his own execution in Rome still fully persuaded that Jesus would return at any moment, an expectation that continues in some Christians of every generation, even if many others secretly think, "Let him come but not in my lifetime."

Holy War hardly was invented by the Covenanters with Yahweh. It is universal, throughout time and place, and doubtless represents what Freud in *Beyond the Pleasure Principle* chose to call the death-drive. I suggest that Yahweh is close to Freud's Reality Principle, so that worshiping him is a kind of reality-testing. Oscar Wilde remarked that life is too important to be taken seriously. Sometimes that suggests the irony of the J Writer, who can hint that Yahweh is too important to take seriously. Yahweh has a dangerous sense of humor. Perhaps Mark's Jesus does also, but not the Lord Jesus Christ.

Aesthetic criteria compel preference for J's Yahweh over the

Tanakh's other versions of God, and for Mark's Jesus rather than those of the other Gospels. Abruptness in J and Mark was transmitted through William Tyndale to Shakespeare's art of surprise. My subject only secondarily is the literary splendor of Yahweh and of Jesus. And yet the power of these figures emanates from narrative characterization and dramatic juxtapositions.

9.

THE TRINITY

THE DOGMA OF THE TRINITY always has been the Church's crucial line of defense against the Judaic and Islamic charge that Christianity palpably was not a monotheistic religion. I shall expound the mystery of the Trinity here, as best I can, while making clear my admiration for its imaginative and cognitive splendor, even as I wonder at its audacity and outrageousness. A mystery, of course, demands faith, and so can only be rationalized, most ingeniously by St. Thomas Aquinas, unless it is irradiated by mysticism in the mode of the Pseudo-Dionysius, the supposed Areopagite (see Acts 17:34), who invented so transcendent a God as to make a mere Yahweh profoundly below the threshold of a mystical name above names and above being—indeed, far above even the Trinity. Mysticism, particularly of this sublime kind, does not belong to the subject of this book, but I cite it here to mark a limit to my argument. In particular, the negative theology of Dionysius, which insisted that language could give no coherent account of the divine, inspired the Eastern Orthodox Church, whose dogmas go beyond those of Western Catholicism and subsequent Protestantism. I turn back therefore to the Western dogma of the Trinity, seeking to uncover it as the structure of anxiety it most assuredly was, is, and always shall be.

Yeshua of Nazareth, descendant of David, habitually addressed Yahweh as father *(abba),* but stopped well short of reducing Yahweh to the single attribute of being "our father who art in heaven." That reduction is Christian, and Yeshua, as we ought never to become weary of recognizing, was not a Christian, but a Second Temple Jew loyal to his own interpretation of the Law of Yahweh. Above all, Yeshua was not a Trinitarian, a statement at once obvious yet also shattering in its implications. American Fundamentalists eagerly anticipate the Rapture, in which Jesus Christ will gather them up into heavenly immortality. That expectation is perhaps central to the American Religion, and is perhaps the most popular poem of our climate, but while sublime it cannot be considered Yahwistic.

The dogma of the Trinity takes for granted that Yahweh already has dwindled into its First Person, God the Father. Even in the work of as profound a scholar as Jaroslav Pelikan, or his precursor Adolph Harnack, no attempt is made to account for the substitution of God the Father for the startling and mischievous Yahweh. The English Romantic poet-prophet William Blake, still inaccurately termed a mystic, saw this with final clarity when he ironically renamed Yahweh as Nobodaddy, nobody's father.

Doubtless one should not ask Trinitarian dogma just who its First Person is, if only because the secret and principal purpose of the Trinity is to justify the displacement of the Father by the Son, the Original Covenant by the Belated Testament, and the Jewish people by the

Gentiles. Jesus Christ is a new God on the Greco-Roman model of Zeus-Jove usurping his father, Chronos-Saturn. The Emperor Constantine, in establishing Christianity as the religion of Roman authority, shrewdly recognized in Jesus Christ a continuation of pagan tradition. Yahweh, like an outworn Saturn, retreated to the remnants of Jewry, until he returned as the Allah of Islam.

With this as a preamble, I turn to the Trinity, Christendom's extraordinary exploit in somehow asserting its innocence as to the exiling of Yahweh. Monotheism may or may not be an advance upon polytheism, but Christianity would not concede its own pragmatic resort to three Gods rather than one. Where and how did the dogma of the Trinity begin? In the fourth century of the Common Era, Athanasius, Bishop of Alexandria, persuaded a majority of his colleagues that Jesus Christ was God, a persuasion both unqualified and yet curiously subtle, since Christ was also man. But what sort of man? Was he a creature or not? The Jewish Christians, led by James the brother of Jesus, had insisted he was, as did Arius, the fourth-century opponent of Athanasius, but the Athanasian Creed won the contest, and Jesus Christ became more God than man, in practice if not quite in theory.

Theology necessarily is a system of metaphors, and doctrine represents its literalization. I am inclined to believe that the best poetry, whatever its intentions, is a kind of theology, while theology generally is bad poetry. Yet theology can be what Wallace Stevens called "the profound poetry of the poor and the dead," and for two centuries now in the United States it has been the poetry of the people. The Trinity is a great poem, but a difficult one, and always a challenge to interpretation. Its sublime ambition is to convert polytheism back into monotheism, which is possible only by rendering the Holy Spirit into a vacuum, and by evading the flamboyant personality of Yahweh. If the Trinity truly is monotheistic, then its sole God is Jesus Christ, not Yeshua of Nazareth but his hyperbolic expansion into the usurper of his beloved *abba*.

The historical Yeshua, insofar as he can be isolated, had his own anguishes of contamination, including toward his immediate precursor, John the Baptist, and also to such forerunners as Abraham, Moses, and Elijah. But he apparently suffered no anxiety of influence in regard to Yahweh, unlike the metaphoric Jesus Christ, whose separate identity demanded the subtraction of all ironic irascibility from Yahweh, who was after all a failure as a father. Oscar Wilde mordantly observed, "Fathers should be seen but not heard; that is the secret of family life." Athanasius, though no wit, may be accounted an ancestor of Oscar Wilde, who, as Borges said, was always right.

AS A LIFELONG CRITIC of poetry, I admire the poem of the Trinity without loving it. If the Trinity is a myth, is it also a dream of love? God the Father, a mere shade of Yahweh, has the primary function of loving his Son, Jesus Christ, and of loving the world so much that he sacrificed Jesus to save it. Yahweh intervened to save Isaac from the overliteralist Abraham, most obedient of Covenanters, but was not available to save Jesus from God the Father. Metaphor runs wild in the Trinity, and with some qualms I enter into its labyrinths now, beginning by quoting the Athanasian Creed, as set forth in 325 at Nicaea:

We believe in one God, the Father of All Governing *[pantokratora]*, creator *[poiētēn]* of all things visible and invisible;

And in one Lord Jesus Christ, the Son of God, begotten of the Father as only begotten, that is, from the essence [reality] of the Father,
[ek tēs ousias tou patros], God from God, Light from Light, true God from
true God, begotten not created *[poiēthenta]*, of the same essence [real-
ity] as the Father *[homoousion tō patri]*, through whom all things came
into being, both in heaven and in earth; Who for us men and for
our salvation came down and was incarnate, becoming human
[enanthrōpēsanta]. He suffered and the third day he rose, and ascended
into the heavens. And he will come to judge both the living and the
dead.

And [we believe] in the Holy Spirit.

But, those who say, Once he was not, or he was not before his generation, or he came to be out of nothing, or who assert that he, the
Son of God, is of a different *hypostatis* or *ousia,* or that he is a creature,
or changeable, or mutable, the Catholic and Apostolic Church anath-
ematizes them.

The target here is the heretic Arius, whose Jesus Christ was created
by God at a particular moment, and so was mutable. Against Arius,
this creed gives us rhetoric that is now familiar yet rather shaky when
it speaks "of the same essence as the Father." There is nothing biblical
about such a formulation, nothing Yahwistic, and yet without it Jesus
might be only a transitional figure rather than the last Word.

A metaphor can be historically persuasive yet still rather desperate, and *homoousion* here is an extravagance still not staled by repetition.
But Jesus and Yahweh are not constituted "of the same stuff," which

is the primary meaning of the Greek *homoousios,* a compound adjective probably taken over by early Christian theologians from the Gnostic heretics. G. L. Prestige, in his useful *God in Patristic Thought* (1936), charmingly compares the Gnostic statement that the primal Adam, or man-god, resembles God as an image but was not of the same stuff, to the piece of marble representing Prime Minister Gladstone in the National Liberal Club:

> It is made of different stuff from that which Mr. Gladstone himself consisted: it is in the image of Mr. Gladstone, but not *homoousios* with him.

And yet the *homoousion* increasingly vexed all the Patristic thinkers (to call them that) as it ought to go on perturbing us, primarily Catholics, though not Unitarians, Muslims, and those Jews who still trust in the Covenant, since none of these give credence to the Trinity. Trinitarians had not clarified the central dilemma of their metaphor, since the Council of Nicaea's Creed does not resolve the question as to the fusion of Father and Son. A metaphor remained a metaphor. Athanasius, however, insisted that Jesus Christ was not creaturely, nor was the Holy Spirit: the Trinity was an identity of substance, and not merely an analogy. But if God is one being, how can he also be three entities, each capable of separate description?

St. Augustine shrewdly relied upon the analogue that a single human consciousness brings together the will, the memory, and the understanding, but that does not resolve the Athanasian tangle. There is a gap between Augustine's Latin culture and the Greek Trinity that an inward turn could not bridge. The Greeks saw one essence and three substances, while the Latins proclaimed one essence, *or substance,* and three persons. For the Latins, the Trinity comprised three subjects; for the Greeks, three objects—but this was largely a linguistic difference, and pragmatically made little real difference.

Tritheism is imaginatively as appealing as any other polytheism, and Latins and Greeks alike had ancestral cultures replete with gods, godlings, and oracles. Yahweh and his prophets just could not be assimilated by the classical world without a transmutation into Gentile forms. Dispassionately I can savor the endless ingenuities of Trinitarianism, just as the equivocal ironies of Plato's theology inspire my reception of his *Timaeus,* which is far closer to Athanasius than it is to I Isaiah. How could it not be? James Joyce's grand comic formula was: Jewgreek becomes Greekjew. For all the Byzantine brilliance so masterfully charted by Jaroslav Pelikan (himself now Eastern Orthodox), Christianity remains polytheistic from the Gospel of John down to the contemporary United States.

WAS THE AGNOSTIC GOETHE accurate in his concession that morally we are monotheists? Our Law is not Hebraic or Greek, but ultimately Roman, and our great chronicler, whom we await, would be an American Edward Gibbon, who will depict our inevitable decline and fall. Gibbon attributed the ruin of the Roman Empire to the triumph of Christianity. Our decay and eventual collapse might be brought about by Republican triumphalism, doubtless grounded upon an amalgam of Fundamentalism, Pentecostalism, and the Mormons, who enforce a monotheistic morality while tacitly retaining Joseph Smith's legacy of a plurality of gods. Trinitarianism is dead or dying in Europe (except for Ireland) and wanes in the United States, where even the not very Yahwistic God the Father hovers in the shadow of the American Jesus.

I return to the subtle Greek Fathers, who smoothed out the contradictions of the Trinity, or at least wallpapered them over. Much the best study here is again Pelikan's *Christianity and Classical Culture* (1993). Pelikan's heroes are the so-called Cappadocians, from the Turkish region north of Armenia Minor and south of Pontus: Gregory of Nazianzus, the brothers Basil of Caesarea and Gregory of Nyssa, and their wise sister Macrina, all of them fourth-century doyens of Hellenized Christian theology. They rightly understood that the Council of Nicaea had failed to formulate a sufficient defense against the accusation that Trinitarianism was a polytheism. Armed with a sophisticated Christian Platonism, they set out to provide exactly this. Pelikan implicitly judged them to have been more successful than Augustine and Aquinas in this Quixotic quest (that last phrase is mine, and not Pelikan's).

Don Quixote was anything but a failure, even if finally he accepted defeat, and Pelikan's Cappadocians were not failures either, because their secret weapon was negative theology, to which I confess a lifelong attachment, and of which Pelikan is the unmatched expositor. This marvelous mode of linguistic negation insists that all language concerning the divine, whether biblical or not, was hopelessly inappropriate, since the transcendental could not be caught in words. Hamlet, unavailable to the negative theologians, might have made them doubt their own procedures, except that Shakespeare's most articulate character breaks through into transcendence only in order to embrace nihilism. What was called the Word was above words, and divine light far outshone natural light. Essentially, negative theology is a metaphorical technique for exposing and undoing metaphor. That is a delight for Hamlet, but a rugged trial for questers who seek the Trinity. Father, Son, and Holy Spirit all are extreme metaphors, whereas the J Writer's Yahweh was a person and a personality, as was Mark's Jesus. Western monotheism, I would argue, has only two persuasive dramatizations of God: Yahweh and Allah. Jesus Christ is a remarkably mixed metaphor, while God the Father and the Holy Spirit are tenuous analogies. The American Jesus is quite another matter, because he is beyond metaphor and has subsumed the national myth of the New People chosen for a future of dreamlike happiness, compounded of emancipated selfishness and an inner solitude that names itself as true freedom. Our vital prophets, Emerson and Walt Whitman, were post-Christian, and so is their nation, since the American Jesus can be described without any recourse to theology.

PELIKAN'S CAPPADOCIANS neatly (perhaps too much so) navigated between Greek polytheism and strict Yahwism by cheerfully admitting that all analogues for the divine were inadequate. If the Trinity was metaphorical, that did not disturb them, since the Christian godhead by definition was passionless. Still, I admire the Cappadocian dance of negations that saves the Trinity, or at least reconciles it with Platonic culture. Christian Platonism dispenses with Socratic irony, at least until the nineteenth century, with the advent of Søren Kierkegaard, whose emphasis began where the Trinitarians ended. How can one *become* a Christian, he asks, in a realm that proclaims its share in Christendom? If Christianity is to involve taking on some of the mystery of the suffering of Jesus, is it attainable when the new believer simply joins herself or himself to most of society? The question would have made little sense in the fourth century and would have oppressed Kierkegaard a millennium and a half later, and seems unanswerable in twenty-first-century America.

Scholars rarely agree as to how and by whom the Trinitarian controversies were resolved. Pelikan champions his Cappadocians:

> The congruence of Cappadocian Trinitarianism, this "chief dogma," with Cappadocian apologetics, was summarized in their repeated claim that the orthodox doctrine of the Trinity was located "between the two conceptions" of Hellenism and Judaism, by "invalidating both ways of thinking, while accepting the useful components of each." Gregory of Nyssa put this claim boldly: "the Jewish dogma is destroyed by the acceptance of the Logos and by belief in the Spirit, while the polytheistic error of the Greek school is made to vanish by the unity of the [divine] nature abrogating this imagination of plurality." In sum, therefore, "Of the Jewish conception, let the unity of the [divine] nature stand; and of the Hellenic, only the distinction as to the *hypostases,* the remedy against a profane view being thus applied, as required, on either side." This apologetic symmetry permitted him to assert: "It is as if the number of the Three were a remedy in the case of those who are in error as to the One, and the assertion of the unity for those whose beliefs are dispersed among a number of divinities." To the heretics who asserted that the Son of God was a creature but who nevertheless worshipped him as God, he posed the alternative of committing idolatry by "worshipping someone alien from the true God," or of falling into Judaism by "denying the worship of Christ." He summarized the same polemical point by accusing this

heretical view of simultaneously "advocating the errors of Judaism and partaking to a certain extent in the impiety of the Greeks," accepting the worst of both while orthodoxy accepted the best of both. (*Christianity and Classical Culture,* 1993, pp. 249–50)

Gently one might observe that more than "Jewish dogma" is destroyed by the Word and the Holy Spirit: where can Yahweh's solitary supremacy be located in this still thoroughly Greek formulation? J. N. D. Kelly, in his *Early Christian Doctrines* (revised edition, 1978), tells us that the Trinitarians' God is "essentially rational." Remembering the J Writer's endlessly surprising Yahweh, I am at first a touch stunned, but a little reassured when Kelly resorts to Augustine for a warier understanding of human limitations in grasping the mysteries of the Trinity:

> While dwelling at length on these analogies and drawing out their illustrative significance, Augustine has no illusions about their immense limitations. In the first place, the image of God in man's mind is in any case a remote and imperfect one: 'a likeness indeed, but a far distant image. . . . The image is one thing in the Son, another in the mirror.' Secondly, while man's rational nature exhibits the trinities mentioned above, they are by no means identical with his being in the way in which the divine Trinity constitutes the essence of the Godhead; they represent faculties or attributes which the human being possesses, whereas the divine nature is perfectly simple. Thirdly, as a corollary from this, while memory, understanding and will operate separately, the three Persons mutually coinhere and Their action is one and indivisible. Lastly, whereas in the Godhead the three

members of the Trinity are Persons, they are not so in the mind of man. 'The image of the Trinity is one person, but the supreme Trinity Itself is three Persons': which is a paradox when one reflects that nevertheless the Three are more inseparably one than is the Trinity in the mind. This discrepancy between the image and the Trinity Itself reminds us of the fact, of which the Apostle has told us, that here on earth we see 'in a mirror, darkly'; afterwards we shall see 'face to face.' (pp. 278–79)

If the three members in the godhead are indeed persons, they are *not* so in our merely human minds. The image and the Trinity itself cannot be reconciled, because now we confront a dark saying, one of the enigmas that Paul could not resolve. Augustine must be the most tendentious writer in the Western world before Sigmund Freud, yet here the great Bishop of Hippo ceases to expound and tells us to take it or leave it, though the leaving will put us in jeopardy. One can see why Pelikan prefers his Eastern Fathers to Augustine, and to Aquinas who comes after, but the issue of Greek polytheism as against Yahwistic or Islamic monotheism has not exactly been resolved. As a mediator between Pelikan and Kelly, I turn back to G. L. Prestige, in 1936. His Trinitarian hero is the totally unknown sixth-century theologian called the Pseudo-Cyril, who invented the metaphor of "co-inherence," or "the form of one God in three Persons and not three Persons in one Godhead." Tritheism could thus be averted, but by a doctrine so intricate and subtle that some exasperation seems in order. Is an indivisible Trinity still a threefold entity? Prestige thinks so, but how far can you go in literalizing a metaphor? I quote Prestige's praise of Pseudo-Cyril out of my desire to be fair, but I wonder what Yahweh could have made of these Greek convolutions. Theology, after all, was invented by the Jewish Platonist Philo of Alexandria, in order to explain away Yahweh's human personality. Here, then, is Prestige on his unknown hero:

> However, once found, it is immensely to our unknown author's credit that he perceived the fruitfulness of its application to the Persons of the Trinity. This was indeed his greatest and wisest innovation. If the conception of interpenetration is forced in relation to the natures of Christ, it is an admirable description of the union of the three Persons of God. And it was necessary to find some such simple and expressive term for the purpose. As has been emphasised already, both ousia and hypostasis, the crucial terms in the doctrine of the Trinity, are concrete. It follows that the doctrine, for the sake of completeness, ought to be capable of being defined from the aspect of either term. From the aspect of a single concrete ousia, expressed objectively in three presentations, the being of God is clearly stated, and monotheism is safeguarded in the doctrine of identity of ousia. But owing at first to the accidents of controversy, and later to the abstract tendencies of the sixth century, the aspect in which God came to be more commonly regarded was that of three objects in a single ousia. The uppermost term is not hypostasis, and it becomes an eminent practical necessity to formulate a definition which, beginning from the uppermost term, will equally well express the truth of the monotheistic being of God. Without such a definition, the recurrence of tritheism was almost inevitable—not because the truth was unknown or unappreciated, but because in the absence of a convenient and illuminative formula the minds of the unwary are apt to be

drawn away from central truths to invent heresies on the perimeter. Nor does 'the unwary' necessarily mean the most obtuse. The ablest minds may be the narrowest. (*God in Patristic Thought,* 296–97)

The "it" in the second line of this quotation is co-inherence, and Prestige is commending Pseudo-Cyril for inventing a better metaphor than any other Trinitarian had employed. But though tritheism is held off, the expense of spirit is at the waste of Christ's humanity. Both Yeshua of Nazareth and Yahweh are irrelevant to the Trinity, since they were not just metaphorical and everything deposited in the Trinity is nothing but metaphor.

10.

NOT PEACE BUT A SWORD OR
DIVINE INFLUENCE

T HIS BOOK'S TITLE employs "divine" both as adjective and
verb, because the names Jesus and Yahweh retain their magical
potency. Indeed, Jews who continue to trust in the Covenant tend to
avoid both names, though for rather different reasons.

At my age, just turned seventy-four, I begin by wondering: what is
my book's genre? A lifelong lover of great literature, I write literary
criticism, but with an admixture of what I have learned to call "religious criticism," where William James is my distant model. I am neither a historical critic of literature nor of religion; a student of
Emerson, I regard criticism as allied more to biography than to the
myths we call "history." Yet the biography either of Jesus or of Yahweh cannot be composed. Jack Miles did his lively best in *God* and in
Christ, but that double biography culminated in God's suicide, and
Yahweh is hardly given to *that* crisis. Eclipse, self-exile, wily evasiveness
all are Yahwistic proclivities, but suicide? Never.

"Jesus" in my title primarily means Jesus-the-Christ, a theological God. Yahweh, in his earlier and definitive career, is not at all a theological God, but is human, all-too-human, and behaves rather unpleasantly. Christianity transforms Jesus of Nazareth, a historical person about whom we possess only a few verifiable facts, into a polytheistic multiplicity that replaces the uncannily menacing Yahweh with a very different God the Father, whose Son is the Christ or risen Messiah. Both of these divinities are shadowed by a ghostly Paraclete (Comforter) named the Holy Spirit, while Miriam, the mother of the historical Yeshua or Jesus, lingers nearby under the designation of "The Virgin Mary."

The American Jesus stands somewhat apart from this pragmatic polytheism because he is the primary God of the United States, and has subsumed God the Father in what I continue to suggest we call "the American Religion." This Jesus has a burgeoning rival in the Holy Spirit of the Pentecostalists, and perhaps our future will see divided rule between these somewhat disparate entities. All this matters because Christianity wanes in Europe (Ireland excepted) and is exemplified primarily in the Americas, Asia, and Africa, competing in those latter continents with Islam, which now becomes more militant than at any time since its aggressive inception.

Yahweh is the protagonist of the Tanakh, which is distinctly *not* identical with the Old Testament. Jesus Christ is the protagonist of the New, or Belated, Testament, which revokes the Covenant between Yahweh and Israel. Politicians and religious figures (are they still separate characters?) speak of the Judeo-Christian tradition, but that is a social myth. It would make about as much sense if they spoke

of a Christian-Islamic tradition. There are three rival so-called mono-
theisms, but the Jews are now so tiny in population, compared with
the Christians and Muslims, that they could vanish all but completely in another two generations, three at most. This book therefore is not a polemic favoring Yahweh over his usurper. Perhaps it is,
in part, an elegy for Yahweh. If he has vanished, he still ought to be
distinguished clearly from Jesus-the-Christ and even from Allah, who
in some respects does remain closer to the God of Abraham and Isaac,
Jacob and Ishmael, and Jesus of Nazareth than do the Christian
deities. I am aware that these truths are scarcely welcome, but what
truth is?

A quest for the historical Yahweh (so human that at times he behaves like a person) is as self-defeating as the endless quests for the human or historical Jesus. Invariably, the quester discovers herself or
himself, since pragmatically the individual's identity is profoundly involved. How could it not be? After a lifetime spent in the company of
scholars both great and small, I go on learning daily that their "objec-
tivity" is shallow, and that their "subjectivity" can be deep, which
makes for the authentic differences between them. Where, then, am I
in relation to this book?

As a literary critic whose quest, these last forty years, has been for
some secrets of the dynamics of the influence process, I find myself
prepared to examine the most important instance of it, the Greek
New Testament's anxiety of influence in regard to the Hebrew Bible,
the Tanakh. Just as the Christian Bible, quite aside from including the
New Testament, is distinctly not identical with the Bible of the
Covenant between Yahweh and Israel, there is not one single Chris-

tian Bible: Catholics, Eastern Orthodox believers, and Protestants vary in their inclusions and exclusions. As I have noted, all of them significantly change the sequence of the Hebrew Bible so that it ends with Malachi, the final minor prophet whose name means simply "messenger," and who thus leads up to John the Baptist at the start of the canonical New Testament. The Tanakh concludes with II Chronicles, and a final "let us go up" to the rebuilding of Jerusalem and the restoration of Yahweh's Temple.

READING THE NEW TESTAMENT through from start to finish is a very mixed aesthetic and spiritual experience, whether one reads the original Greek text or the most powerful English translation, William Tyndale's, or else the Revised Standard Version, from which my quotations are drawn, unless otherwise indicated. I remember being unhappy with Northrop Frye's literary criticism of the Bible, in his books *The Great Code* and *Words with Power,* primarily because the Tanakh continued its captive status in Frye, and was interpreted as a foretelling of the New Testament. When I remarked this to Frye, he gruffly replied that Anglo-American literature was founded upon that foretelling. Yet Frye was mistaken: from Shakespeare to Faulkner, the Hebrew Bible is not subsumed by the New Testament. John Milton, like William Blake and Emily Dickinson a radical Protestant sect of one, from Frye's viewpoint would have to be considered a Judaizer of the Bible. *Paradise Lost* gets Jesus on and off the Cross with unseemly haste, in six words broken in half by an enjambment: "so he dies,/But soon revives." A disciple of Frye in my youth (we broke apart, intellectually but not emotionally, on my formulation of the anxiety of influence), I remain startled at finding in Frye's posthumously published *Notebooks* his reaction to the Gospels:

> I find the Gospels most unpleasant reading for the most part. The mysterious parables with their lurking & menacing threats, the emphasis placed by Christ on himself & his uniqueness & on a "me or else" attitude, the displaying of miracles as irrefutable stunts, & the pervading sense of delusion about the end of the world—those are things for intellectual ingenuity to explain away, & the fact that they're there recurrently comes to me out of the delicate tissue of rationalization. The Christian Church with all its manias had started to form when the Gospels were written, & one can see it at work smoothing things away & making it possible for Christianity to be kidnapped by a deformed & neurotic society. I wonder how long & how far one can dodge or resist the suggestion that the editorial shaping of Scripture is a fundamentally dishonest process.

Many readers of the Gospels—probably most—would disagree with Frye. Since I have no personal investment in the Gospels, I neither agree nor disagree. Nothing I ever have read, and go on rereading, except perhaps for St. Augustine, is as tendentious as the Gospels: they have a fixed design upon the reader, and as churchly propaganda may have little to do with the historical Yeshua of Nazareth. We never will know. The Gospels give us a Jesus as mythological as Attis, Adonis, Osiris, or any other dying and reviving divinity. A Messiah who is God Incarnate, and dies on the Cross as an Atonement for all human sin and error, is irreconcilable with the Hebrew Bible.

Only by a strongly creative misreading of the Tanakh could so immense a disparity have been redressed. The New Testament is held together by its revisionist stance toward the Hebrew Bible. A considerable splendor ensues from this revisionism, whether one is comfortable with it or not. The persuasive force of the Gospels, and of the entire New Testament structure, testifies to the power of an imaginative achievement, riddled with inconsistencies, but more than large enough to have weathered its self-contradictions, including a Jesus whose mission intends only Jews as beneficiaries, and disciples who address themselves only to Gentiles. What could Yeshua of Nazareth have made of Martin Luther's outburst "Death to the Law!" which in many German Lutherans who served Hitler became "Death to the Jews!" The Germans would not have crucified Jesus: they would have exterminated him at Auschwitz, their version of the Temple. No less than Hillel, Jesus affirmed the Torah, Yahweh's teaching and Covenant.

JON D. LEVENSON'S BOOK *The Hebrew Bible, The Old Testament, and Historical Criticism* (1993), lucidly centers upon a distinguishing realization:

> To say that the Hebrew Bible has complete integrity over against the New Testament is to cast grave doubt upon the unity of the Christian Bible. It is like saying one can read the first ten books of the *Aeneid* as if the last two did not exist, and this, in turn, is to say that the last two add nothing essential: the story can just as credibly end without Aeneas's slaying Turnus. Now for Christians to say that the New

Testament adds nothing essential to the Hebrew Bible is on the order of Marxists saying that they have no objection to leaving the means of production in the hands of private capitalists: the assertion belies the speakers' announced identity. (p. 101)

The Chinese Communists continue to affirm their Marxism while relying upon capitalism to increase prosperity, but since they hold military power, the contradiction is pragmatically meaningless. Christian theologians are (happily) no longer allied to state power, yet their adherence to the shibboleth of "Judeo-Christian tradition" needs more clarification than some are willing to give to it. If the two traditions were not radically different, the remnants of Jewry, endlessly assaulted, would now have dissolved. Jews remain stubborn, partly so as not to yield to force and fraud, partly because of something in the numinous intensity of Yahweh that somehow will not wholly diminish. Jews, according to an eloquence of Tony Kushner's, have tumbled from the pages of books. Those books—the Tanakh, the two Talmuds of Babylon and Jerusalem, and all the subsequent commentaries down to this moment—have a cumulative strength that defies time and its afflictions.

(2)

Robin Lane Fox, a properly skeptical historian, in his *The Unauthorized Version* (1992), insists "we can be certain" that no biblical text existed, as we have it now, before the eighth century B.C.E., but I disbelieve him.

E. A. Speiser, an extraordinary scholar, in his *Anchor Bible Genesis,* dates the earlier layer of Genesis, Exodus, Numbers to the tenth century B.C.E., the time of David and Solomon. The Yahwist, or J Writer, composed that magnificent early strand of what was fused with other texts by the author-editor who put together the Genesis-to-Kings sequence during the Babylonian Exile. Fox rightly takes this sequence as fiction, not truth, but biblical history is rarely "truth" in the restricted sense sought by professional historians, whose rhetoric allows only a rather reductive kind of truth. Whether or not one trusts in the Covenant, or believes that Jesus was the Christ, or submits to Allah by accepting Muhammad as the seal of the prophets, it scarcely is useful to reduce Yahweh to a truth/fiction choice. If Yahweh is a fiction, he is much the most disturbing fiction the West ever has encountered. Yahweh is, at the least, the supreme fiction, the literary character (to call him that) more endless to meditation than even Jesus Christ, or the most capacious Shakespearean characterizations: Falstaff, Hamlet, Iago, Lear, Cleopatra. J is Yahweh's Shakespeare but hardly God's inventor.

The early career of Yahweh precedes any narrative we possess, which stimulates imagination. I muse on Yahweh and desire to know his foreground, and why it took so long for him to name himself. We get to know his varied personalities (I count seven) but always remain puzzled as to his character. Perhaps he was puzzled too, before he named himself Yahweh. After all, he had absorbed several other gods and godlings, and a certain dyspepsia is one of the consequences.

We do know what he looks like, even though he forbids all portraiture of him. He looks like us, or rather we look like him, having been created in his image. Kabbalah and its antecedents tell us he is enormous, the cosmic King Kong of deities. Jack Miles says of God that he talks to himself; I would add that Yahweh never *overhears himself,* as though he were someone else. He is not therefore a Shakespearean character, and Shakespeare sensibly kept him offstage. Yahweh, who is not a Narcissus, might seem one. Richard II is a narcissist; Hamlet is not. By definition, Yahweh cannot, like Richard II, feel sorry for himself. Neither can the Yahweh-like King Lear, whose furies cross over into madness. Yahweh, who suffers fiercely from any ingratitude, and is desperately jealous, crosses over to insanity during the forty years of leading the Israelites through the Wilderness, in the crazy trek from Egypt into Canaan. A generation dies out and their children reach the Promised Land. Moses himself, Yahweh's prophet, is shown the land but refused entrance to it. Yahweh, who generally is bad news, is the worst possible news when he ends Moses. But then, he has been a personal disaster for Moses from the start. I regret suggesting that he has been a disaster for his champions more often than not, but that is the long story of the Tanakh, and of most Jewish experience since. If one doubts the Incarnation (even St. Paul did), then the Mel Gibsonian recently renewed debate as to the guilt of the Jews, rather than the Romans, can be set aside. Yahweh is guilty.

(3)

When Yahweh, many centuries later, became the God of Protestant Reformation, he was regarded as saying to each Protestant, "Be like me, but do not dare to be too like me." The Yahweh of the J Writer need give no admonition except that we must refrain eating from the Tree of Life, which would make us immortal. Theodore Hiebert, in *The Yahwist's Landscape* (1996), shrewdly observes that this would have been eternal life on earth, rather than in some realm beyond. J's Yahweh likes to walk in the cool of the day, in the Garden of Eden, and enjoys a picnic with Abraham. Jesus, who gives himself to wine and hearty eating when he can, is never more like Yahweh than in such feasting. Nietzsche's "Think of the earth" is Yahwistic, since J's Yahweh is wonderfully anthropomorphic, as when he himself closes the door of Noah's ark or buries Moses in the soil with his own hands. Most significant, Yahweh fashions Adam out of the *adamah,* moist and rich red earth. Homer superbly shows us war between gods and men; the J Writer goes beyond that, portraying theomorphic men and women, who walk and talk with Yahweh. Briefly, J's Yahweh is not a sky god, but alternates between cultivated fields and mountaintops.

Frank Cross emphasizes the storm god aspect of Yahweh, but only as a battle music heralding the divine warrior who subdues the sea (Pharaoh) and the earthly enemies of Israel. Though he will undergo a remarkably nuanced series of maturations, Yahweh begins as an ambivalent creator and destroyer, like Shelley's West Wind. But before adumbrating his qualities as a fighter, I want to grant myself an excursus to describe Yahweh's most surprising quality, his uncanniness.

He is not primarily a trickster god, and does not always delight in mischief, though he certainly indulges himself when he confounds the would-be builders of the Tower of Babel. But he creates all things, including the category of the unexpected. The genius of the J Writer, which bursts through the palimpsest of Genesis-to-Kings, refuses confinement. There are no boundaries to Yahweh, which is why his

Blessing is best defined as the gift of more life on into a time unbounded. Heaven on earth is his promise; *his* Kingdom decidedly is of this world. Hiebert notes that Yahweh is neither omniscient nor omnipresent; he has to go off to investigate matters for himself.

Though immortal, Yahweh has aged, and perhaps he is too old to care anymore. I do not have in mind Yahweh's appearance as the Ancient of Days in the Book of Daniel, which William Blake ironically transformed into aged Ignorance, or "Old Nobodaddy aloft." What impresses me most about Muhammad's Allah is that he continues to care, much too ferociously, which is why Islam remains perpetually militant. Christianity's God the Father cares, yet he is a diminishment of Yahweh, and is lacking in personality. Such a waning is necessary, in the fourfold pantheon he shares with Jesus Christ, the Holy Spirit, and the Blessed Virgin Mary. *The Muslim Jesus* (2001), as edited by Tarif Khalidi, is a key to the difference between Allah and God the Father. The Qur'an assigns Jesus a unique place as the prophet who directly anticipates Muhammad, but this is a Jesus stripped of all Christianity and "cleansed" of Incarnation, Crucifixion, Atonement, and Redemption. Only the Ascension remains to distinguish Jesus from previous prophets, though in Shi'i thought and subsequently in Sufism the ascensions of Enoch and of Muhammad's grandson Hussayn are related to a Gnostic Jesus—the Angel Christ, as he sometimes is termed. Jesus does not die but ascends to Allah, and abides with Allah in order to be present at the Ending (hinted at in Qur'an 43:61). But then, Qur'an 61:6 presents Jesus as announcing the coming of Muhammad as the seal of all prophecy. Allah crucially is appeased when in Qur'an 5:116 he fiercely asks Jesus whether he and Mary are two gods aside from God, and Jesus gently replies that he has said no such thing.

There are no Judaic texts in which Yahweh asks Jesus for a similar disclaimer, but we could hardly expect that. I return to the earlier, bellicose Yahweh, whose warrior personality is most flamboyant in the Book of Joshua, 5:13–15, where the Redactor softens what is clearly a stunning epiphany of Yahweh himself about to go into battle at Jericho:

> Once, when Joshua was near Jericho, he looked up and saw a man standing before him, drawn sword in hand. Joshua went up to him and asked him, "Are you one of us or of our enemies?" He replied, "No, I am captain of the Lord's host. Now I have come!" Joshua threw himself face down to the ground and, prostrating himself, said to him, "What does my lord command his servant?" The captain of the Lord's host answered Joshua, "Remove your sandals from your feet, for the place where you stand is holy." And Joshua did so.

The Tanakh is a cavalcade of memorable episodes, but this manifestation of Yahweh as swordsman always stays with me. The drama of this moment is adroit. Joshua, commander of Israel, does not recognize the soldier and boldly demands, "Are you one of us or of our enemies?" Yahweh replies as himself, not merely as angelic captain, with "Now I have come!" and Joshua, requesting orders, is told precisely what Moses receives in Exodus 3:4–6, the warning that to stand in Yahweh's presence is to stand on holy ground, sandals removed. Abruptly, the Book of Joshua proceeds to the siege of Jericho, and

Yahweh dictates the crumbling of the city's walls. One does not again see the Christian God the Father with drawn sword in hand.

(4)

Though Yahweh's personality and character are not its overt subject, I find useful for meditating upon Yahweh the incisive and compact *Sinai and Zion: An Entry into the Jewish Bible,* by Jon D. Levenson (1985). Ancient Israelite religion centers upon Mount Sinai, where the Torah was given by Yahweh, and Mount Zion, where the Temple was built for Yahweh by Solomon. Levenson notes the truth that a major difference between Talmudic Judaism and biblical religion is that the rabbis had the Bible as their focus, after the Temple was destroyed. The two mountains, of Covenant and of Temple, bring together Moses and David, Yahweh's prophet and Yahweh's adopted son. Yahweh's choice of the high places is not gratuitous, because as warrior he descends from mountains to battle his enemies. His Temple, as Levenson shows (following Ezekiel in particular), is spiritually identical to the luxurious Garden of Eden, where he delighted to walk in the cool of the day. When Eve and Adam are expelled from the Garden, lest they become gods, it goes on existing, guarded by Cherubim. By implication, the destruction of Yahweh's Temple, whereas on Sinai he ate in common with his people, was also the obliteration of Eden, never available to us again unless the Temple is rebuilt. But if the Bible itself replaces the Temple, then the book stands in also for the Garden, which may be why Akiba so passionately insisted that the Song of Songs, which is Solomon's, had to be canonical.

Unable any longer to walk in Eden or feast in his Temple, Yahweh resides in the Jewish Bible. So comfortably is he at home there that he needs no Third Temple, unless by now (as it seems to me, though not to those who trust still in the Covenant) he has exiled himself even from the delight of its pages.

PART II. YAHWEH

11.

THE DIVINE NAME:
YAHWEH

THE FOUR-LETTER YHWH is God's proper name in the
Hebrew Bible, where it appears some six thousand times. How
the name was pronounced we never will know: Yahweh is merely surmise, because oral tradition guarded the sacred name. Elias J. Bickerman, in an immensely useful essay, "The Historical Foundations of
Postbiblical Judaism" (published in 1949), and now most easily available in *Emerging Judaism,* edited by Michael E. Stone and David Satran
(1989), establishes that after Alexander the Great's conquest of Palestine, in 333 B.C.E., the usage of the Divine Name underwent changes.
Already, after the fifth-century B.C.E. return from Babylon, the Name
was taken to be magical and was not to be pronounced. Instead God
was called by either Elohim (divine being or beings) or Adonai (my
Lord). The arrival of the Greeks, who called God Theos, stimulated
the Jews to refer to him as Kyrios, Greek for Adonai or Lord.

Bickerman traces to Greek influence the rise of a new Jewish intel-
ligentsia, secular scribes, essentially civil servants, administrators, and

business advisers, for whom Yahweh was a name both archaic and for-bidden. By the time of Hillel and Jesus, you could live out a full life space without ever hearing God's actual name. Since the meaning of the name is as obscure as its pronunciation, this may have been just as well.

Yahweh must be a very old name; it is used in Deborah's great War Song (Judges Chapter 5), which is eleventh-century B.C.E. and could be the oldest text in Hebrew. There are references to the name as early as 1400 B.C.E. in Syria. I myself doubt the myth that Moses first ac-quired Yahweh's name by marrying the daughter of Jethro the Kenite (Exodus 3:1), because the voice of Yahweh punningly proclaiming his true name (*ehyeh asher ehyeh*—"I will be where and when I will be" or "I am that I am") reverberates with such extraordinary authority in Ex-odus 3:14. Something with the aura of what must have moved an-cient Israelites is evoked when God insists upon his proper name, which is the foundation for his Covenant with the Chosen People.

All of us, sooner or later, muse upon our own name, sometimes ruefully. Yahweh is never rueful in affirming his true name, almost as though he himself felt the charismatic force and magical suggestive-ness of that opening "Yah." Consider how startled we would be if someone were introduced to us as "Yahweh" Jones or Shekhinah Smith. The other day, in New York City, I endured a telephone dis-pute with two florists named Jesus and Muhammad, while scarcely reflecting upon their names. Yahweh has a somewhat different effect, at least upon me. Allah (a variant on Elohim) appears to have suffered little loss in numinosity of name since the composition of the Qur'an. Perhaps the most active of numinous names today is Satan, who after all is nearly as prominent in the New Testament as Jesus is.

12.

YAHWEH ALONE

Unlike Jesus', Yahweh's characteristic ways of speaking are not primarily enigmatic. The grand exception is his *ehyeh asher ehyeh,* the punning self-naming to which I return throughout this book. Jesus, we can assume, understood this terrifying definition of the will of God better than we can. I do not doubt the Gospels when they show us a Jesus who invariably addresses Yahweh as *abba,* Aramaic for "father." Jesus longs for Yahweh, and for Yahweh alone. In Platonic terms, the love of Jesus for God the Father is *eros* and not *agapē* (which becomes *caritas* in Latin, and our "charity"), because *eros* is the desire for someone superior to the self while *philia* is love between equals and *agapē* is love of a higher being for a lesser one. If you accept some variety of Christianity, however, then the love of God directed by Jesus is *caritas* and not longing. In the contemporary United States, where Jesus either replaces Yahweh or is fused with him, we easily get this mixed up. Whatever anyone wishes to see in the affection of Jesus for the Beloved Disciple, frequently identified with the author of the

Gospel of John, or for Mary Magdalene, it is more sensible to regard such attachments as charity, and not *eros.*

I do not believe that the personality of Jesus can be understood without some prior comprehension of the personal qualities of Yahweh. Theologians from Philo of Alexandria down to the present have attempted to obscure Yahweh's frequent appearance in the Hebrew Bible as a theomorphic human. Fortunately, theology fails when confronted by the J Writer's Yahweh, whose closest literary descendant is Shakespeare's King Lear, at once father, monarch, and irascible divinity. W. H. Auden found Shakespeare's Christ in Falstaff, a challenging though inaccurate discovery. The riddling Hamlet has touches of William Tyndale's Jesus, but Falstaff is the brother of his historical contemporary, Chaucer's Wife of Bath, another enthusiastic sinner. Had Hamlet encountered the ghost of King Lear as his father's spirit, Shakespeare's art could have given us an authentic entrance into the longing of Jesus for Yahweh. Whether or not Nazareth regarded Jesus as illegitimate we cannot know, but I find it simplistic to reduce the love of Jesus for Yahweh to a search for an absent father. Jesus was a rabbi, which still means a teacher, and he taught Torah, though with swerves from it very much his own. He came not to abolish but to fulfill the Law, however fiercely St. Paul, Martin Luther, and many since have labored to misapprehend this subtlest of all teachers, whose ironies transcend even those of Plato's Socrates. Socrates was not a Platonist, and Jesus was not a Christian. He would not tell who he was, and none of us—Christians, Muslims, Jews, or secularists—are ever likely to know what only Yahweh knows.

(2)

Who was, who is Yahweh? He certainly keeps telling us, but all of the Tanakh, Talmud, Kabbalah, New Testament, and Qur'an together never can suffice to encompass all we are told, and yet not told. My long experience of reading Shakespeare, and teaching others to read him, has made me distrust all approaches to him, since he *contains* us. Owen Barfield noted that we could experience dismay when we came to realize that what we regarded as our own emotions frequently first were Shakespeare's thoughts. Historicizing Yahweh seems to me even more useless than historicizing Shakespeare. Whether or not you believe that God made you is a secondary matter here. Primary is our continued need for authority to sanction the self's sometimes desperate yearning for a mode of transcendence. Adam B. Seligman, in his *Modernity's Wager* (2000), accurately states our current impasse in the sociology of religion: "a God that can be grasped, a God that can be conceptualized is not a God" (35). When, in earlier books, I have called Shakespeare "a mortal God," my intention was to confront the ungraspable Hamlet, who defies all our conceptualizations. Even more does Jesus, but no one is as beyond our apprehension as is Yahweh. Whether you regard him as "a literary character" or as your creator scarcely matters in this struggle to reach the unreachable. I gain little when historians of religion accurately inform me that Israel's original god was El, who later was identified with Yahweh. I commend Mark S. Smith's admirable *The Early History of God* (1990) for students of Yahweh's relations to ancient Israel's various godlings, but history is only one mode, and Yahweh is beyond any representations except those of the Tanakh at its strongest. Witness Milton's God in *Paradise Lost,* not only the great blemish on an otherwise magnificent epic, but also absurdly inadequate when contrasted to Yahweh as rendered by the J Writer, the Psalmists, and the Prophets.

One learns to shrug off references to "cultic rituals" and "cultic sites" in regard to Yahweh. The very phrase "cult of Yahweh" has an aura of the ridiculous. Two other terms that to me appear equally opaque are "monotheism" and "anthropomorphism." Yahweh is a person and a personality; the godlings of Canaan are bric-a-brac, while Yahweh is Divine Man and beyond that, and his favorites— Abraham, Jacob, Moses, David—are also theomorphic. David's lineal descendant, Joshua of Nazareth, is at the least theomorphic in ways that transcend the subtle complexities of his precursors.

Yahweh's own complexities are infinite, labyrinthine, and permanently inexplicable, despite the extraordinary skills at interpretation of the Sages of the Talmud and Kabbalah, and of the Sufi masters who confronted the Qur'an, where Yahweh speaks the entire work, as Allah, voicing the full range of God's reactions to our failures in *submission* to his will. We can be maddened by Yahweh's bewildering turns at revealing and concealing himself, particularly since, in Torah and Qur'an alike, his furies can seem so sudden and capricious. Yahweh commands a recalcitrant Moses to descend into Egypt, and then attempts to murder his prophet at a night encampment in the Negev, on the way down. And we can cease all dispute as to guilt for the Crucifixion: Yahweh sacrifices Jesus, and indeed forsakes him, at least in this world.

Gnosticism, whether you choose to regard it as a religion or as only a tendency, was provoked, by precisely these aspects of Yahweh, into what Hans Jonas characterized as an ecstasy of unprecedentedness.

This strong response to an overwhelming literary strength was a rebellion against both the Tanakh and Plato, and produced the Gnostic
Jesus, celebrated by William Blake, the greatest of English poet-
prophets in the wake of John Milton. William Butler Yeats, the most
eloquent of all Anglo-Irish poets, carried Blake's argument into the
twentieth century, though without Blake's love for the figure of
Jesus.

Yahweh is hardly to be dismissed as Blake's "Old Nobodaddy" or as
James Joyce's "hangman God." Either we are transcendent entities or
merely engines of entropy, and Yahweh, with all his ambivalences,
marks the difference between the two possibilities, at least in cultures
that derive from Hebraism and its Hellenizing, including the rival religions of Judaism, Christianity, and Islam and their subsequent, only
partial secularizations. If Shakespeare contains us (and he does), then
Yahweh contains Shakespeare, whether the poet-dramatist himself
was recusant Catholic, Protestant, Hermetist, or inaugural nihilist,
uncanny precursor of everything still to come.

YAHWEH, though a frightening ironist, particularly in his rhetorical
questions, is even more frequently given to hyperbole, the figure of
excess or overthrow. Jesus, himself an astonishing master of irony,
emulates Yahweh in the hyperbolical demands of his teaching, with
insistence upon perfections that mere humans scarcely can achieve.
Rhetorical excess in Jesus seeks to persuade us to yield up easier
moralities for more difficult ethical choices, for what might be called
the Sublime awareness of others at the expense of our all-too-natural
selfishness. Since Jesus, unlike Christianity, never asserted he was the

Messiah, his hyperbolical ethics are all the more unnerving. Can Yahweh and Jesus be one in this regard, since the Law, despite St. Paul's
misreading of it, does not ask us for perfection? The Pharisees made
that clear, and if Jesus sometimes argued with and against them, essentially the disagreements turned upon his fierce yearnings for perfection. That may be why he asserted that he came to fulfill the Law,
and not to abolish it.

JESUS HAD a composite precursor: Abraham, Moses, Elijah, John
the Baptist, but ultimately this discipleship was resolved by the emu-
lation of Yahweh alone. The biblical Yahweh of rugged Galilee was a
starker being than the Temple-inhabiting Yahweh of Jerusalem in
Jesus' time. By the time of Jesus, the willfulness of Yahweh had been
transmogrified into the God's uneasy alternations of presence and absence. There he hovered in the Holy-of-Holies of the Jerusalem Temple, while permitting the Romans to occupy his Chosen People's
land, and to carry out tens of thousands of crucifixions of Zealots and
other Jews even before the Revolt of 70 C.E., in which the Temple was
destroyed. I am wary of psychobiography as an approach to Jesus,
even when the genre of Erik Erikson is developed as responsibly as it is
by John W. Miller in his *Jesus at Thirty* (1997). One wants a more com-
prehensive and literary kind of biography, such as Jack Miles's adroit
portrait. But the strong misreading of Yahweh by Jesus, when he insists upon human perfection, of father by son, is something different
from either psychohistory or literary biography. If Christ was, as Jack
Miles said, "a crisis in the life of God," then Jesus, not yet resurrected,

could only be his own internal crisis. There is, though, the Gnostic Jesus of Valentinus of Alexandria, a Jesus concerning whom the Valentinians affirmed, "First he resurrected, and *then* he died." This brilliant but difficult formulation suggests that we emerge into true life only by a mystical transformation that long precedes our dying. That is closer to my concerns in this book than are the approaches of Miller and of Miles. Whether or not Jesus resurrected after his death is crucial to Christianity, indeed constitutive of it, since only such a resurrection might validate the faith that Jesus became the Christ—that is, the Messiah.

As I understand the Transfiguration, where Jesus appears as a third with Moses and Elijah, this vision justifies the Gnostic and Sufi contention that Jesus first became "the Angel Christ" and only after *that* resurrection did the Nazarene return to the human condition and, presumably, die upon the Cross. I venture "presumably" because of the Gnostic and Muslim insistences that Simon the Cyrene, who carried the Cross, was crucified instead of Jesus. There are other traditions, even more esoteric, that the Roman soldiers were bribed, and that Jesus was taken down from the Cross, still alive. By Jewish Law, which he accepted, he had been defiled, and after appearing to his disciples and to his brother James the Just, he underwent recuperation and then chose exile, passing across the Jordan into the land of Nod, in Cain's tradition. Other legends say that Jesus wandered on, following the track of Alexander the Great's legions, until at last he came to Hellenistic North India. There, as precursor of the Muslims, who still acclaim him as a prophet surpassed only by Muhammad, the Nazarene sage lived out the peaceful old age of a gentle Gnostic Jew, perhaps musing upon the ironies of his divinization by the Christianity he had not sought to found.

(3)

Even that fanciful Jesus must have continued his lifelong meditation upon his father, Yahweh, who may have lost interest in a prodigal son who already had fulfilled the paternal purpose. Christianity overdetermines and overexplains that purpose, by seeing Jesus as the fulfillment of God's eternal plan. As I am a Jew (however heretical) and not a Jewish Christian, I am compelled to remain puzzled as to God's purpose. Jack Miles is a former Jesuit, like the formidable F. E. Peters, author of the masterly *The Monotheists* (2004), but Miles intrigues me in ways very different from my fascination in absorbing Peters on the contests between Judaism, Christianity, and Islam. Miles asks the disconcerting question-of-questions about Yahweh and Jesus: "Rather than a further development of God's character, does Jesus, the Lamb of God, not seem its terminal collapse?" (*Christ,* 252). "Yes, he does," Miles insists, and as a strictly literary judgment, that seems to me beyond dispute, because Jesus wants a more perfect God than Yahweh ever could be. But I want to turn back to the enigmas of Yahweh's character, not so much in disagreement with my earlier meditation on Yahweh's personal psychology (*The Book of J,* 1990, 279–306) but with a heightened awareness of Yahweh's own anxieties of influence.

Kierkegaard is the lion in my path, because his Nebuchadnezzar, after ceasing to be a grass-eating beast, marvels at Yahweh:

And no one knows anything of Him, who was His father, and how He acquired His power, and who taught Him the secret of his might.

If Nebuchadnezzar were speaking of Jesus, the answer might seem to be Yahweh, but I wonder at that also. John the Baptist taught Jesus (uncomfortable as that makes the Gospels), and like Elijah, the Baptist appears to have known the secrets of the Merkabah, Yahweh's chariot as seen and described by Ezekiel. Yahweh is an admonisher and not a teacher: that role he assigns to Moses and Isaiah, to Hillel and Jesus, to Akiba and Muhammad. Kierkegaard's Nebuchadnezzar is the epitome of the Danish ironist's sense of the immense difficulty of *becoming a Christian* when you dwell in Christendom. The unfathered Yahweh is our hopeless dilemma: Who was *his* teacher? How can we know anything at all about Yahweh?

(4)

We have the Tanakh, and the Sages who interpreted it in the two Talmuds, of Babylonia and Jerusalem, and in commentaries upon them. Commentaries are akin to the sequence of plays within plays within plays that crowd *Hamlet,* from Act II, Scene 2 through Act III, Scene 2. The mind of Yahweh is more intricately labyrinthine than that of Hamlet, infinitely so, but the enigmatic Prince of Denmark remains the most advanced instance of a purely literary representation that we know. Yahweh's Shakespeare, the J Writer, manifested an irreverence that sparked the defensive rise of theology, which is always an effort to explain away the human aspects of God (or of Jesus). I prefer Kabbalah to theology as a guide to Yahweh's personality, and I will experiment also with some Kabbalistic forays into the nature of Jesus, though not following the precedents of Christian Kabbalah.

THE EARLIEST STRAND of Torah centers upon Yahweh, who is a rather different personage from Christianity's God the Father and from Islam's Allah. The J Writer's Yahweh is intimate with us, close by, while the Christian God the Father has retreated into the heavens. And Yahweh knows his limits (which may spur his irascibility), but Allah possesses total powers. There is a curious trade-off here. As God's might augments, his presence wanes. Yahweh walks and talks with men and with angels: he sits under the terebinth trees at Mamre, devouring a meal prepared by Sarah, and he picnics on Sinai with seventy-three elders of Israel. I cannot envision Allah or God the Father molding a mud-pie figurine out of the red clay, and then breathing life into it. If Yahweh is uncanny, he also is as canny as Jacob, who wins the new name of Israel. Mischievous, inquisitive, jealous, and turbulent, Yahweh is fully as personal as a god can be. Allah's dignity does not permit such descents into human vagaries.

The great rabbis of the Talmud tend more to emphasize our merited fear of God than his corporealization as Yahweh, a numinous name they strictly decline to employ. Instead, the Sages multiply descriptive epithets and alternative names with a zest that displays ingenuity, albeit with a touch of desperate inventiveness. Any sensible participant in the Covenant fears God, who at once proclaims his particular care for Jewry and pragmatically demonstrates a malign neglect of his people. Tony Kushner follows distinct aspects of Jewish tradition in *Perestroika,* where the angels sue Yahweh for desertion, but the sophisticated divinity retains Roy Cohn as unbeatable counsel for the defense. Shall we say that Yahweh is overambitious and therefore overworked?

FEARING YAHWEH IS SENSIBLE. Is there any basis for loving him? Or is such love only a training to join what Christianity called its martyrs, the "athletes of death"? Yahweh expects both: love where there is fear, and fear where there is love, a destructive fusion when taking place between persons, but appropriate in regard to him alone. Each of us needs to decide whether that is proper either for the Original Covenant, or for the Belated one, or whether instead to submit to Allah. Reject all three, and you are a secularist, humanist, or nihilist, or a Gnostic who dismisses William Blake's Nobodaddy. There may be other options, imported from Asia, but Buddhism does not come easily to me.

(5)

Is there a difference between the love for God, and for women and men, when we compare the Talmudic Sages and Jesus? Plainly there is, and it is a difference that truly makes a difference, but then there are Sages and Sages. Jesus was frequently and formidably ambivalent toward all but a few persons, and not unsurprisingly he lacked the patience of the great Hillel, who resisted every eschatalogical impulse.

Ephraim E. Urbach, in his authoritative *The Sages: Their Concepts and Beliefs* (1987), concedes the severity of Shammai and the apocalyptic intensity of the aged Akiba, who encouraged the disaster of the Bar Kochba rebellion against the Romans. Hillel, though, gave a new understanding of the Torah by virtue of the fact that he was both saintly and humble. His saintliness found expression in the testimonies to his acts, which were all for the sake of heaven, and to his absolute trust in God, which left no room for misgivings or fears.

The attributes of humility, patience, love of one's fellows, and the pursuit of peace, which Hillel displayed, did not diminish the stringency of his ethical and religious demands, or prevent him from placing full responsibility on man, whom he required to act for his own perfection and for the public weal. Man is obliged to make endeavors, for "If I am not for myself, who will be for me?" But he cannot achieve much through seclusion and separation, and he must remember, "And being for my own self, what am I?" Nor may he forget that his time is limited and he dare not procrastinate—"And if not now, when?" (*Sayings of the Fathers*, I.14). Man's relations with his fellow man were defined by Hillel not only in the rule attributed to him as a reply to the proselyte who asked to be taught the whole Torah while standing on one foot—"What is hateful to you do not do to your fellow"— the like of which the would-be proselyte might also have heard from others, but in the demand that one must not pass hasty judgment on the actions of another person, just as one is forbidden to be confident of one's own righteousness. The principle is "Be not sure of yourself until the day of your death, and judge not your fellow until you come into his place" (*Sayings of the Fathers*, II.5). However, a man's humility and self-criticism are no excuse for keeping aloof from the community. Hillel even instructs the Sage who has acquired the qualities of saintliness and humility, "Sever not yourself from the community . . . and where there are no men strive to be a man" (*Sayings of the Fathers,* II.5–6).

POPULAR MISCONCEPTIONS of Jesus place him far closer to this humane gentleness than he actually was. Hillel did not carry a sword of consciousness but rather peace, and only peace. St. Paul's misprisions as to letter and spirit, Law and love, are obliterated by bringing together Hillel and Jesus. For Hillel, the holy spirit had passed from prophets to the community of Israel, and a remnant of Sages spoke to the community, and did not seek to work miracles. Nor did they attempt to abolish Sanhedrin and Temple, though they spoke out against all malfeasances in administration. I understand Confucius only a little, yet he and Hillel had their affinities. Hillel did not, like Jesus, divide the populace into sheep and goats, but desired rather to make all Israelites into "associates," partners in the ongoing Redemption, not in the far-off Coming of the Kingdom of Heaven. It is sentimentalism to seek a reconciliation between Hillel and Jesus, however well-meaners desire this. Hillel indeed said, "Where there are no men strive to be a man," rather than an incarnation of God. If I can find any bond between Hillel and Jesus it would be in the Sage's "Be not sure of yourself until the day of your death, and judge not your fellow until you come into his place." Perhaps I myself need to reflect more on that than I tend to do.

(6)

Yahweh, "anthropomorphic" in the J Text underlying the Torah, is only in part transcendentalized by the Sages. Ever since it was republished in 1968 I have been deeply influenced by Rabbi Arthur Marmorstein's three-volumes-in-one, *The Doctrine of Merits in Old Rabbinical Literature* and *The Old Rabbinic Doctrine of God,* divided into *Names and Attributes* and *Essays in Anthropomorphism.* Zwi Werblowsky, introducing these splendid books, bluntly dismisses "arrogant Christian prejudice," which used to find in the Sages mostly "Pharisaic" self-righteousness swept away by Jesus and by Paul. So usefully fierce is Werblowsky that I happily quote him:

> *Shamayim*—a metonymy for "He who dwelleth in Heaven"—no doubt carried overtones of a transcendent, omniscient, numinous God, though not necessarily of a far-away God who is remote from all human concerns. The latter idea, ascribed to the rabbis by, e.g., Bousset, is again one of the vain conceits fondly invented by gentile scholars in order to persuade themselves that Judaism was a religion without vitality and warmth, and devoid of any sense of the nearness of God (and man's nearness to Him). Even more fanciful is the more recent discovery that the phrase "our father in heaven"— which, to an unprejudiced mind, would seem to evince a certain sense of intimacy with God—still exhibits the remoteness of a transcendent God. According to this view the ordinary Jew would at best say "my father" *(abi)*, whilst only Jesus could address God with the more intimate word *abba.* It is hardly necessary to discuss

these theories seriously in view of the material assembled by Marmorstein. (p. xiii)

The paradox of presence and absence, as tragic for the Sages as for Jesus, is that Yahweh surpassingly is unpredictable. You can encounter him in the next bush, or he can hide himself when most needed. He may not accept your sacrifice, or may turn away from it. St. Paul insists that Jesus' self-offering as Lamb of God was accepted, but who can ever know? Judaism emphasizes trust in the Covenant, Christianity professes faith that Jesus himself was the New Covenant, Islam is submission to the will of Allah, but trust, faith, submission are none of them knowledge. Gnosis—whether Kabbalah, Christian mysticism, or Sufism—relies upon a knowing and a being known, but that is hardly the epistemology of Aristotle and of Hume.

Marmorstein, with profound immersion in the Sages, understood that the paradox of Yahweh's simultaneous nearness and distance had never been resolved. According to the Talmudists, Yahweh's gradual withdrawal into transcendence is compensated for by the visual (if intermittent) radiance that the Talmudists name as the Shekhinah, an identification vastly expanded in the Kabbalah. The older rabbinic doctrine calls the Shekhinah the ongoing presence of Yahweh in the world, where once he willed to be here, there, and everywhere. Yahweh is incomprehensible without the Shekhinah. If the "beauty of Israel" (2 Samuel 1:19) indeed was the giving and reception of the Law on Mount Sinai, then that beauty was visible only in the Shekhinah. Has Yahweh deserted us? Rabbi Abba bar Mimel, one of the earliest Amoraim, quotes Yahweh as saying, "I am named according to my acts." What were these acts during the twenty ostensibly Christian centuries? Where can we see those acts today? A God who hides himself is one matter, but a Yahweh who dwindles down into an occasional burst of radiance no longer merits the name of Yahweh, which after all primarily must mean being present.

Jesus, however he intended to be interpreted, clearly was present during the actual year or so of his ministry, but was Yahweh ever present to him? The Gospel of John famously has Jesus affirm, "Before Abraham was, I am." Yet Abraham talked with Yahweh, face-to-face, as had Enoch, and nowhere does the New Testament directly confront Jesus with Yahweh, not even in the Transfiguration, where a luminous Jesus is seen with Moses and Elijah, both of them on intimate terms with Yahweh. Moses perishes by God's kiss, and is buried in an unmarked grave dug by Yahweh's own hands, while Elijah ascends directly into heaven without the initial necessity of dying. Since Christian theology from Paul onward insists that Jesus becomes God only in and through the Resurrection, there remains little puzzle for believers in the rather remote relationship of the living Jesus to Yahweh. Jesus, so far as we can tell, believed that his heavenly Father at least visited the Holy-of-Holies, on Yom Kippur, the appointed Day of Atonement. Yet why is it that not once, even according to the Christian Testament, was there any face-to-face confrontation between Yahweh and his Son? Why are the Patriarchs and the Prophets so much more directly involved with the presence of God? If Abraham, Moses, and Elijah are more theomorphic men than was Jesus, ought not the New Testament to offer us some explanation? Or is Jesus incarnate Yahweh from birth, as theology wishes us to believe?

Prophecy had ceased in Israel after Malachi, "the Messenger," but only the Muslims regard Jesus as the prophet prior to Muhammad, Seal of the Prophets. Something is again missing here, though Christian theology has declined dealing with this curious absence.

(7)

Mark Twain, hardly a believer, observed that "the Christian's Bible is a drug store. Its contents remain the same, but the medical practice changes." Those contents, it is time for me to observe, are *not* just the Greek New Testament dragging along behind it that captive prize of the Gentiles, the Hebrew Old Testament. The Tanakh decidedly is rearranged, as well as strongly misread, by Christianity. Since the Tanakh is the Book of Yahweh, that means he too is revised by Paul, by the evangelists, and by all the theologians who have sailed in their wake for two millennia. And if Yahweh thus ceases to be Yahweh, what is to be made, then, of a Yahweh Incarnate?

From Augustine through Aquinas down to our squalid, multimedia present, responses flood us, but the question remains as unanswerable as the Book of Job's "Where shall wisdom be found?" Neither Yahweh nor Jesus is responsible for Jerry Falwell, let alone for the mass murderers who have invoked Christianity and Islam as their inspirers. The puzzle of Jesus of Nazareth always will remain. Is he the anointed consciousness of the Gospel of John, who seems always to have known that he incarnates Yahweh, or is he the far more problematical protagonist of the Gospels of Mark and of Matthew? The

Jesus of Mark, in particular, uncannily quests for the origins of his sense of self, unlike the doom-eager hero-god-victim of John.

Jaroslav Pelikan, concluding his massive, superb five-volume cavalcade *The Christian Tradition,* comes to a troubled rest (purely my interpretation, not his) with the Second Vatican Council of the Roman Catholic Church (1962–65). A generation later, I note that Pelikan himself is now a member of Eastern Christendom, and finds in "Eastern Orthodox ecclesiology" a hallowing free of the "authoritarian and juridical" tendencies present both in the Roman Church and in mainline Protestantism. The late Hans Frei used to puzzle me by his gentle prophecy that the spiritual future of Christianity had to involve a return to its Judaic origins. I am hardly a normative Jew, being Gnostic in my deepest self, yet my awe of the religion of Akiba never abandons me, and I have never finally been able to understand either Pelikan or Frei, both of them sublimely normative sensibilities. The paradox of Christianity always will be its conviction that Yahweh, most unsettling of all entities, whether actual or fictive, could in any sense have fathered Jesus of Nazareth, who might have been profoundly disturbed by what latecomers have reworked as his role.

Whoever you are, you identify necessarily the origins of your self more with Augustine, Descartes, and John Locke, or indeed with Montaigne and Shakespeare, than you do with Yahweh and Jesus. That is only another way of saying that Socrates and Plato, rather than Jesus, have formed you, however ignorant you may be of Plato. The Hebrew Bible dominated seventeenth-century Protestantism, but four centuries later our technological and mercantile society is far more the child of Aristotle than of Moses. Jesus, even had he been Yahweh Incarnate, could not have apprehended or comprehended a globe that might seem to him a world under water, already drowned, as if even Yahweh's first covenant, with Noah, had never been cut.

Discoursing on Jesus is closer to considering Hamlet than to meditation upon Shakespeare. Even the richest of Shakespearean characterizations—Hamlet, Falstaff, Iago, Lear, and Cleopatra—seem clear when we contrast them to the total Jesus of the New Covenant. Whom can Jesus talk to, intimately, when he would speak of his own self? Yahweh presumably befriends Abraham and Moses, and finally adopts David, because even God's isolate splendor cannot continue for all eternity. Jack Miles eloquently expresses the pathos of Yahweh's predicament, and thus risks censure of all those, of whatever monotheism, who are uncomfortable with a God not perpetually transcendent.

(8)

As I have mentioned, John Milton allows only six words in *Paradise Lost* to the death and resurrection of Jesus Christ. Incarnation and Atonement did not interest Milton the poet, nor are they central to the major traditions of Western poetry since the European Enlightenment of the seventeenth century. Wallace Stevens, the principal American poet since Walt Whitman and Emily Dickinson, in his "Sunday Morning," contrasts "silent Palestine, / Dominion of the blood and sepulchre" to a Nietzschean dance of "boisterous devotion to the sun, / Not as a god but as a god might be." When I was younger, I sometimes would see graffiti scribbled in the New York City subway system proclaiming, "Nietzsche is dead! God lives!" That has affinities with many

American school boards that decree the teaching of Creationism as against Darwinian evolutionism. If Yahweh is still alive, he perhaps has withdrawn into himself.

(9)

It is an old adage that all of us receive the God we deserve. Whether we deserve a Yahweh so irascible, vengeful, and even murderous is, however, another matter. Crusaders choose to forget that Yahweh himself tortures and executes Jesus, by high design, if credence is to be given to the Gospel of John. What is the human guilt that Jesus must expiate by Yahweh's torture of him, and by similar crucifixions of hundreds of thousands of other Jews by the Roman occupiers? I begin by dismissing St. Paul's and St. Augustine's apologies for God: in Adam's fall, we sinned all. The great Sages of the Talmud held no such barbaric doctrine, a Hellenic importation from the myth of the fire-bringer Prometheus tormented by a sadistic Zeus, and ultimately the Orphic shamanistic story of the revenge of Dionysus upon those who first had torn apart and devoured that infant god. Yahweh is the least self-conscious of all divinities, ever, but Jesus, particularly in the Gospel of John, is a miracle of heightened self-consciousness, implicit model for Hamlet, Shakespeare's lonely tower and apotheosis of self-awareness. St. John's Jesus as God Incarnate is not compatible with the Hebrew Bible, but Christians oddly defend this absolute incongruity by asserting an equal discontinuity between Torah and Talmud, which historically is not an invalid point. A Yahweh who invents death is hardly a Yahweh who subsequently commits suicide, unless you want to make the Tanakh into an ironic tragedy, which is what the embittered author of John's Gospel accomplishes. No text fulfills another, yet there are revisions and revisions: the Talmud adumbrates, which is one mode; St. John instead inflicts an Orphic *sparagmos,* or rending apart, upon the Torah, scattering Yahweh's limbs as though the Master of Presence was another Osiris, or a contemporary Israeli blown apart in a bus by a Palestinian suicide/homicide bomber. St. John, for Yahweh, is bad news.

(10)

Our earliest and defining portrait of Yahweh is by the J Writer, who still seems to me likely to have been an aristocratic woman who wrote in the Age of Solomon, while experiencing nostalgia for Solomon's heroic father, David, ancestor of Jesus, who should indeed have been the King of the Jews, leading them in their hopeless uprising against the Roman imperialists.

I have written about Yahweh at length before, in *The Book of J* (1990), but fifteen years of reflection prompt me now to revise somewhat my earlier vision of the enigmatic God of alternating presence and absence. Hegel, who prompted all of German Protestant theological scholarship, dominated Gerhard Von Rad, whose influence I could not escape in *The Book of J.* Jack Miles playfully suggested that I go ahead and name the J Writer Bathsheba the Hittite, queen-mother of Solomon, a notion I gladly adopted in *The Western Canon* (1994) and again in *Genius* (2002). The extraordinary detachment of the J Writer in regard both to Yahweh and the Patriarchs fits the perspective of a Hittite woman who had married David and given birth to Solomon, and perhaps rendered her own self-portrait in Tamar, who outwits Judah and, by him, becomes the ancestress of David, Solomon, and ultimately of Jesus of Nazareth.

Hegelian-based biblical scholarship frequently founds itself upon an opposition between a Canaanite worship of nature and the Hebrew emphasis upon Yahweh, whose acts constitute history. I recalled in *The Book of J* that the Yahwist had no nostalgia for nomadism, that he walks firmly upon agricultural ground. That is reinforced for me by Theodore Hiebert's *The Yahwist's Landscape* (1996), which points out that there is no linguistic antithesis in ancient Hebrew between "nature" and "history," and rightly assigns to J's Yahweh an altogether earthly realm. His own earth is Adamic, and for Yahweh we need envision no heaven. As I have noted, he is not a sky god, but a planter of gardens, and is happy to picnic in the shade of a terebinth tree. To call Yahweh anthropomorphic is a redundancy. No God has been more human.

(11)

Can we imagine a direct conversation between Yahweh and Jesus? If Christianity is true, how can such an exchange not have taken place on earth, as presumably it would in eternity? If they were two persons, but one substance, surely they knew each other? Or are they two separate Gods, each antithetical to the other, as in some ancient heresies? Christ, by definition, is both God and man, but so, more surprisingly, is Yahweh, who prefers shade to excessive heat, has a fondness for outdoor meals, and is a fierce warrior (sometimes anonymous, as when he appears to Joshua). Since Yahweh is a battler, and Jesus chooses not to be, we could again recall King Hamlet and the Prince of Denmark, who like Jesus is quite pugnacious enough, but also declines to lead men into war. One cannot establish a difference between Yahweh and Jesus merely in their blending of human and divine identities.

But again, why do they not converse, granted that fathers and sons universally face difficulties in communication? The voice of Yahweh is heard in the Synoptic Gospels at both the Baptism and the Transfiguration, in order to affirm that Jesus is his beloved son, but the audience is constituted by ourselves, the readers, as Raymond E. Brown authoritatively emphasizes. The disciples do not seem to absorb the information on either occasion, and evidently Jesus does not need it, and certainly does not respond. Yet again, something appears to be missing. Can it be that *we* are the only privileged audience of the Gospels, except for John's? The disciples seem to have been chosen by Jesus not for their intellects but for ruggedness, particularly Peter, a personality that everyone would now call Rocky, a role in films about Christ that seems apt for Sylvester Stallone. With the others, Peter tends to get everything wrong, as Paul was to complain at a later moment.

We cannot ascribe any personality to the Holy Spirit, but no one would say that Yahweh and Jesus were two personalities yet one substance. I think that the shared uncanniness of Yahweh and Jesus does not extend to the way they speak. Yahweh is too irascible for any extensive reliance upon riddles and parables, while Jesus surpasses Hamlet in enigmatic wit. Perhaps the verbal styles of Yahweh and Jesus are simply too different for conversation to be possible. Even Shakespeare would have smilingly demurred had we asked him to give us a dialogue between King Lear and Prince Hamlet. Where do Jesus and Yahweh most differ? Even in Mark, who is closest to J, Jesus never could say that nothing was impossible for him. He cannot perform miracles in Nazareth. In John he speaks as Yahweh: "Before Abraham was, I am." But John is quasi-Gnostic, and even proto-Sabellian, the heresy that the Son fathers himself.

THE DESPAIR OF JESUS cannot be equated to the desertion of Yahweh (or should we speak of Yahweh's voluntary self-exile?). If Jesus said that the Kingdom of God is within us, was that a hint that God now only exists within us? If a great charismatic master of oral tradition speaks to us only in ironies and dark stories, then Socrates could be the Savior, as he was for Plato and Montaigne. Set aside Paul and John, and regard Luke with a clear eye as to his Hellenism. The Jewish Jesus of Mark and of Matthew is not Yahweh incarnate, but rather a singular and belated prophet, like the Baptist, and prophecy indeed had ceased among the children of Abraham. Out of the strong came forth not sweetness but a sword, or rather two swords, Christian crusading, now centered in the American Religion, and its foe in Wahhabi Islam.

Could we imagine King Lear as Prince Hamlet's father? J's Yahweh in some respects resembles Lear; Mark's Jesus is one of Hamlet's precursors. Imagining J's Yahweh as the father of Mark's Jesus baffles my experience of pondering high literature, where fathers and sons diverge but do not exist in different spheres of being. Theology, itself a compound of Plato and Aristotle, can imagine anything, since persuasive representation is not one of its burdens. But Scripture is closer to Shakespeare than to philosophy. And the paradoxes of a suicidal God are more suited to Athenian tragedy than to Tanakh. This intimates that Christ is Hellenistic while Jesus (in Mark and Matthew) is Jewish. Paul is the puzzle. Jesus is hardly his concern until Easter, the Resurrection. Yahweh did not say, as Paul's Christ did, that the last enemy to be conquered would be death. He is the God of the living; Christ, in yet another enigma, is God of the dead. Who is Jesus? Neither Yahweh nor Christ. Jesus Christ is a new God, even as Christianity was a New Covenant.

Believers, scholars, politicians all deny this, but Western monotheism has become a profound puzzle. I am inclined to argue that Jesus Christ, Allah, and Yahweh all are antithetical, one to another. Father Raymond Brown warns us not to underplay the human in Jesus, but pragmatically believers have reduced that human to Gibsonian floggings. The American Jesus is flawless, as he is in the Gospel of John.

A human cannot be *physically* resurrected from death, and nothing in the Hebrew Bible argues otherwise, where Enoch, Elijah, and Elisha go up directly to Yahweh without dying. St. Paul's understanding of the Resurrection of Jesus was that it was altogether spiritual, but that is not the view of the Gospels or of Acts, where Jesus (except in Matthew) is raised both spiritually and materially. Since Jesus himself has raised Lazarus and others back into the body, as Elijah and Elisha did before him, presumably he is capable of doing the same for himself.

Consider the J Writer's Yahweh in this context, or rather can he be so considered? Jews and Muslims alike say "No!" God does not allow himself to be humiliated, whether by Romans, Germans, or Americans. A crucified Yahweh (as in Miles) is oxymoronic. That could be Odin hanging on the world-oak to gain knowledge of the runes, but Yahweh, as I have remarked, is not a dying and reviving God. Christology is a weird science from the perspective either of Judaism or of Islam. Immersing myself in its study has been an educational experience for me, not at all akin to my bafflement when I try to absorb Buddhism or Hinduism, both of which evade me. With Christology, I cultivate patience, since always I seek the answer to one question: how can Yahweh be seen as accepting mortality, even as another road to reassuming his prior status and function? The Christological reply is that God chose to become love, at whatever cost. Father Raymond Brown, speaking with the authentic voice of Christology, tells us there was no other way by which the divine generosity toward humankind could be manifested.

W. H. Auden disapproved of Prince Hamlet on Christian grounds, arguing that the most gifted character in modern Western literature loved neither God nor other humans, nor even himself. Aristotle observed that complete solitude was possible only for a beast or a god, and perhaps Horatio, one loyal follower, holds Hamlet back from the category of godhood, which would destroy the play.

As a Catholic priest, Brown properly insisted that "if Jesus is not the 'true God of true God,' then we do not know God in human terms." And yet we certainly do know an all-too-human Yahweh in the J Writer's portrait of an anxious, pugnacious, aggressive, ambivalent God, who had fallen in love with King David, displaced by J into her depiction of Joseph as surrogate for the fascinating warrior-king who had fathered Solomon. Like all but a few Catholic scholar-priests,

Brown seems to find in Yahweh only a theological God, a kind of heavenly university president rather than a man of war.

The Synoptic Gospels are not theological tractates but stories, highly ambiguous on the matter of the godhead of Jesus. It was not until 250 years later, at the Council of Nicaea, in 325 of the Common Era, that Jesus was designated "true God of true God." In Mark 10:18, Jesus declines to be praised as a "good teacher" on the grounds that "No one is good but God alone." Paul in I Corinthians 8:6 takes care to distinguish between the "one God, the Father" and "one Lord, Jesus Christ." One could multiply instances, but theologians in reply go on citing textual variants, intricacies of syntax, and a handful of passages that are not so much suspect or equivocal as they are tendentiously staged. The most famous is the Gospel of John 20:28, when Jesus appears a week after Easter, and the disciple Thomas alludes to Psalms 35:23: "My God and my Lord." But John notoriously begins with the very different identification of the Word with God, and *logos* is a very misleading translation of the Hebrew *davar,* which is at once a word, a thing, and an act. Yahweh is a name and so a word, and he is always the essence of act, and hardly to be described as a supreme thing in a cosmos of things. The Synoptic Gospels place Jesus within that category. The Yahweh of the J strand in Torah is too dynamic to be contextualized, precisely because *davar* has no equivalent in Greek.

What would be the consequences—for religion, culture, and society—if Christianity, of any denomination, ever acknowledged that it worships two, or three, or even four Gods (Yahweh, Jesus, the Holy Spirit, and Mary) rather than one? Islam, from its beginnings, has regarded Christianity as a polytheism, though it honors Jesus. Historically, the Church judged Islam to be a Christian heresy, even as the second-century rabbis rejected Christianity as a Jewish heresy. And yet I wish to bring a different perspective, a pragmatic one, to the consideration of arguments about divinity: are we not, in many ways, all of us polytheists, in crucial aspects of our lives? By that "we" I mean not only Jews, Christians, and Muslims but also secularists, agnostics, even declared atheists. Americans are necessarily postpragmatists, as Richard Rorty has observed: only differences that make a difference truly matter in the United States. Would an acknowledgment that monotheism no longer exists make such a difference?

Let me juxtapose two sages—Goethe and Freud—in their varied attitudes toward religion. Goethe saw himself as more a god than a Christian, while Freud asserted he was a godless Jew. Expressing homage to Jesus, Goethe scorned Paul and all of Christianity after him. With Catholic Vienna all around, Freud tactfully refrained from psychoanalyzing Jesus, while finding in Moses a precursor, whose monotheism represented a progressive advance for culture, by way of renunciation of the drives. There is a curious leap in Freud's identification with the man Moses, which has little rational basis. Freud liked to think of himself as a spiritual *conquistador,* with Moses as one of his forerunners, though precisely why monotheism, in Freudian terms, was a human triumph I simply cannot know. If you want Freud's self-image, confront the Moses of Michelangelo, a sculpture that to Freud was an icon.

Visions of leadership by definition are agonistic; they compete with one another for the unique place, high beyond all others. The Hebrew Bible offers Moses, David, and Elijah as its instances. It is odd that the New Covenant has to deal with the embarrassment of John the Baptist, whom Jesus began by following. Nevertheless the Christian Bible has defeated and refashioned the Tanakh, and Jesus Christ subsumes Abraham, Moses, and David, while Elijah and his avatar in John the Baptist are reverently set aside. The Western vision of leadership centers upon Christ, from Constantine until the Renaissance, when Machiavelli and Shakespeare, whose Hamlet is a counter-Machiavelli, pragmatically disturb the center. Freud's lasting importance, I venture, has less to do with the science of mind than with the images of leadership in the West. Jesus, Machiavelli, Shakespeare, and Freud are a curious fourfold, but our captains of politics and industry often blend the four, generally with only a limited awareness of their mixed heritage. Yahweh, archaic and exiled, has yielded leadership to his usurpers.

Where, now, are we to locate the Yahweh who was the charismatic of charismatics, who defined leadership in ways utterly alien to Homer and to Confucius? Though no public figure, for good reason, will say so overtly, the war against terror remains a belated repetition of the wars of Yahweh. Our second invasion of Iraq was the unhappiest of replays, even a parody of the Crusades. Machiavelli, reduced to a popular caricature from the English Renaissance onward, is still the Messiah of geopolitical realism, prophetically outlined in *Thoughts on Machiavelli* (1958), by Leo Strauss (1899–1973), oracle of the neocons who persuaded George W. Bush to launch his Baghdad Crusade. Strauss is eloquent in summing up Machiavelli's replacement of "religion" by "prudence":

> It is impossible to excuse the inadequacy of Machiavelli's argument
> by referring to the things he had seen in contemporary Rome and
> Florence. For he knew that the notorious facts which allowed him to

speak of the corruption of Italy proved at the same time the corruption of Christianity in Italy. It is somewhat worthier but still insuffi-
cient to excuse the inadequacy of Machiavelli's argument by the
indescribable misuse of the Biblical teaching of which believers in all
ages have been guilty. At any rate, many present-day readers who
have some understanding of the Bible are likely to be less shocked
than amazed by Machiavelli's suggestions. They have become accus-
tomed, not only to distinguish between the core and the periphery of
the Biblical teaching, but to abandon that periphery as unnecessary
or mythical. Machiavelli was unaware of the legitimacy of this distinction. Recent theology has become inclined to deny that divine
punishment is more than the misery which is the natural or necessary consequence of the estrangement from God or of the oblivion of
God, or than the emptiness, the vanity, the repulsive or resplendent
misery, or the despair of a life which is not adherence to God and
trust in God. The same theology tends to solve the difficulty inher-
ent in the relation between omnipotence and omniscience on the
one hand and human freedom on the other by reducing providence
to God's enabling man to work out his destiny without any further
divine intervention except God's waiting for man's response to his
call. Machiavelli's indications regarding providence are concerned
with that notion of providence according to which God literally governs the world as a just king governs his kingdom. He does not pay
any attention to the fact that the prosperity of the wicked and the afflictions of the just were always regarded by thinking believers as an
essential part of the mystery of the providential order. We almost see
him as he hears the saying "all they that take the sword shall perish
by the sword" and answers: "but they who do not take the sword

shall also perish by the sword"; he does not stop to consider that only the first, by appealing to the sword, submit entirely to the judgment of the sword and therefore are self-condemned, seeing that no mixed body is perpetual.

We perish by the sword whether we take it up or not, but what has happened to the terrible swift sword wielded by Yahweh in wars all his own? The Shakespearean question to ask Yahweh would be "What have you promised yourself?" In the Christian view, since Jesus is the Son of God, that translates into the rhetorical question "What did Yahweh promise Jesus?" In *Hamlet,* as Julia Lupton subtly shows, the Prince is an anti-Machiavel in parrying Claudius, and yet still an English Machiavel himself, subordinating love to fear as the most reliable means of inducing obedience. Yahweh pragmatically is indifferent to whether he is loved or feared, because either love or fear yields sacrifices as emblems of our obedience, a praxis that culminated in the apparent death of Jesus.

Jews and Christians no longer sacrifice animals upon altars of blood, but Yahwism dispensed with animal sacrifice only when the Romans obliterated the Temple, and Christians continue it, in sublimated form, by the communion in which bread and wine are emblematic of the flesh and blood of Jesus. Sacrifices in the ancient mode, supposedly abolished, are enacted daily in religious violence throughout the world, in organized terror, and in war, which is little else. Simone Weil blamed all this on the Hebrew Bible, while amazingly she fused the Gospels and the *Iliad* as "poems of force" that did not sanction ritual slaughter. Achilles, greatest of killing machines, could not have comprehended Simone Weil, but then I confess that I also cannot.

SACRIFICE IS, to me, the most unpleasant of subjects, but a book centering on the Divine Names, Jesus and Yahweh, hardly can evade the material that the Redactor, exiled in Babylon, wove into his Genesis-to-Kings structure by incorporating the Priestly source, so different in every way from the Yahwistic narrative. J ironically evaded sacrifice, despite the Aqedah incident (the word "aqedah" means "binding"), in which Abraham almost sacrifices Isaac to Yahweh, in the ultimate model for the slaughter of Jesus as the Lamb of God.

So vexed a subject is Yahwistic sacrifice that no modern scholarly authority has matched its semicondemnation by the magnificent Sage of the twelfth century of the Common Era, Moses Maimonides, who in his *Guide for the Perplexed* insists that it was at best a secondary matter for the divine will. Maimonides relies upon the prophetic tradition, particularly as exemplified in Samuel's rebuke to Saul:

> But Samuel said:
> Does the Lord delight in burnt offerings and sacrifices
> As much as in obedience to the Lord's command?
> Surely, obedience is better than sacrifice,
> Compliance than the fat of rams.
> For rebellion is like the sin of divination,
> Defiance, like the iniquity of teraphim.
> Because you rejected the Lord's command,
> He has rejected you as king.
>
> I SAMUEL 15:22–23

Maimonides also cites Isaiah 1:11–13 and Jeremiah 7:21–23:

"What need have I of all your sacrifices?"

Says the Lord.

"I am sated with burnt offerings of rams,

And suet of fatlings,

And blood of bulls;

And I have no delight

In lambs and he-goats.

That you come to appear before Me—

Who asked that of you?

Trample My courts no more;

Bringing oblations is futile,

Incense is offensive to Me.

New moon and sabbath,

Proclaiming of solemnities,

Assemblies with iniquity,

I cannot abide."

Thus said the Lord of Hosts, the God of Israel: "Add your burnt offerings to your other sacrifices and eat the meat! For when I freed your fathers from the land of Egypt, I did not speak with them or command them concerning burnt offerings or sacrifices. But this is what I commanded them: Do My bidding, that I may be your God and you may be My people; walk only in the way that I enjoin upon you, that it may go well with you."

Why did the prophetic rejection of sacrifice not forestall the apparent sacrifice of Jesus? There is an ambivalence in the rabbinical Oral Tradition that I myself would trace to the movement from a human Yahweh who enjoys feasting (as evidently Jesus also did) to an increasingly transcendent God who required no nourishment beyond praise and obedience.

Unless you are a consistent vegetarian, you cannot convince even yourself of your own sincerity in deploring animal sacrifices in so many of the world's religions throughout time. But since only a few of us, presumably, are cannibals, human sacrifice is rather a different matter. That makes child sacrifice one of the horrors-of-horrors, including the more than a million children slaughtered by the German people in Hitler's Holocaust.

I turn here to another study by Jon D. Levenson, *The Death and Resurrection of the Beloved Son,* subtitled *The Transformation of Child Sacrifice in Judaism and Christianity* (New Haven, 1993). Levenson's argument, to me persuasive, finds the ultimate source of the sacrifice of Jesus in Yahweh's initial command that Abraham immolate Isaac. The Aqedah studied by Levenson is narrated in Genesis 22:1–19, and always renders me very unhappy, despite the brilliant defense offered for it by Kierkegaard in *Fear and Trembling,* one of his ironic masterpieces. Kierkegaard interprets Abraham as the Knight of Faith who nevertheless understands that Isaac will survive. That understanding is more Lutheran than Judaic, and Levenson clearly distinguishes it from the exegesis of Rashi (eleventh century C.E.), who reasoned that Abraham the prophet foretold his son's escape. Rashi is merely sensible, whereas Kierkegaard reinvents the ancient Christian idea of "the absurd." Abraham, according to the Qur'an, was a Muslim, but only

Kierkegaard regards Abraham as a Christian before the fact, as it were: "He believed by virtue of the absurd; for there could be no question of human calculation, and it was indeed the absurd that God who required it of him should the next instant recall the requirement."

I come to the conclusion that most of us misunderstand what Yahweh means by "love" and "fear." E. P. Sanders in his *Jewish Law from Jesus to the Mishnah* (1990), page 271, makes a splendidly helpful observation:

> We now make a great distinction between "inner" and "outer," and those of us who are Protestants, or heirs to the Protestant tradition, distrust external forms. It should be remembered that, to ancient Jews, "love thy neighbor" and "love the stranger" were not vague commandments about the feelings in one's heart, but were quite specific. "Love" meant, "Use just weights and measures"; "Do not reap your field to the border, but leave some for the poor"; "Neither steal, deal falsely nor lie"; "Do not withhold wages that you owe"; "Do not take advantage of the blind or deaf"; "Do not be biased in judgement"; "Do not slander"—and so on through the verses of Leviticus 10 and many others.

Leviticus 10 presumably is a misprint here for 19:9–17:

> When you reap the harvest of your land, you shall not reap all the way to the edges of your field, or gather the gleanings of your harvest. You shall not pick your vineyard bare, or gather the fallen fruit of your vineyard; you shall leave them for the poor and the stranger: I the Lord am your God.
>
> You shall not steal; you shall not deal deceitfully or falsely with

one another. You shall not swear falsely by My name, profaning the name of your God: I am the Lord.

You shall not defraud your fellow. You shall not commit robbery. The wages of a laborer shall not remain with you until morning.

You shall not insult the deaf, or place a stumbling block before the blind. You shall fear your God: I am the Lord.

You shall not render an unfair decision: do not favor the poor or show deference to the rich; judge your kinsman fairly. Do not deal basely with your countrymen. Do not profit by the blood of your fellow: I am the Lord.

You shall not hate your kinsfolk in your heart. Reprove your kinsman but incur no guilt because of him. You shall not take vengeance or bear a grudge against your countrymen. Love your fellow as yourself: I am the Lord.

You shall observe My laws.

Yahweh's love is Covenant-keeping, no more and no less. I don't think Paul got that wrong, but Augustine—for all his greatness—got Paul wrong. Jesus in the Gospel of Mark, so far as I can tell, is Yahwistic in his pragmatic sense of love. In old age, I begin to be daunted by Leviticus, my least favorite book of the Tanakh. It may be that moral benevolence is a better love than most of our passions.

13.

WHAT DOES YAHWEH
MEAN BY "LOVE"?

YAHWEH'S LOVE for the people he chose is Covenantal: therefore conditional and revocable. It is a commonplace of New Testament scholarship to note that Paul and Mark do not set Jesus against the Pharisees; Paul's pride in his Jewishness, and in having sat at the feet of the great Rabbi Gamaliel, is reflected in his respect for the Pharisees, earlier associates, while in Mark's Gospel, Jesus interprets the Law essentially in Pharisaic modes, though with a swerve all of his own. While Paul almost follows Jesus in denouncing divorce between women and men, though Moses had legislated for it, Paul's and Mark's Jesus certainly does not see Yahweh as having divorced his Chosen People.

The largest paradox of Christianity in Luke, John, and nearly all that comes after is the simultaneous dismissal of the Jewish people as obsolete (at the best), while still relying all but totally upon a revisionary interpretation of the Hebrew Bible. When Jesus, in the Transfiguration, appears alongside Moses and Elijah, their presence intimates others as well: Abraham, Isaac, Jacob, Joseph, Elisha, and a shadowy host drawn from their traditions. Yahweh again proclaims Jesus' beloved sonship, at the moment of Baptism, and it is vital that the Son's precursors again be with him.

I cannot recall Yahweh expressing authentic love for anyone, even when in I Chronicles he promises David that, after the hero's death, Solomon will be the recipient of the heavenly monarch's love, as if Solomon were to be God's own son. The implication is that Yahweh has resisted falling in love with David, who might be called the Hebrew Hamlet: poet, swordsman, tragic but exuberantly conscious quester. It is not accidental that Jesus is David's descendant, but through a younger line, not Solomon's.

Yahweh, like King Lear, demands a bewildering excess of love, the frequent stigma of bad fathers. We are not permitted to see Queen Lear, and to speak of a hypothetical Mrs. Yahweh is the blasphemy-of-blasphemies (except for Mormons). Whether we name her Wisdom, the Shekhinah, Eve, or the Virgin Mary, she would become an incestuous daughter, like Lot's daughters, who perhaps were avenging themselves for their father's offering them up to the Sodomites, in order to protect the Angels of Destruction. Clearly, Yahweh (until a new *eros* emerges in the Kabbalah) loves David but only as Lear loves Cordelia, with a tenderness that masks irascibility at its core. Or rather, since Christianity replaces Yahweh with the benign God the Father, First Person of the Trinity, the qualifications fade away from that tenderness.

This gap between Yahweh and the Trinitarian God the Father is another demonstration that Judaism is not Christianity's parent. Rather, Judaism and Christianity are enemy brothers, both stemming from Second Temple Judahisms, a truth most people of goodwill try to evade. As there are well over a billion and a half Christians, and perhaps only fourteen million or so self-identifying Jewish survivors, that makes for rather more than a hundred Christians to each Jew. Yahweh's injunction to his Chosen, "Be fruitful and multiply," is a horrible irony on a globe in which the Jews form less than a tenth of one percent of the world's population. That is about the proportion of the Mormons in the universe, but the Mormons have a dynamism of growth, while the Jews continue to dwindle. Pragmatically, Christianity and Islam, and the religions of Asia, will inherit whatever earth the American Republican plutocracy allows to survive the stripping of ecology. I am compelled to conclude that Yahweh has exiled himself from the Original Covenant, and is off in the outer spaces, nursing his lovelessness.

Baruch Spinoza's magnificent admonition has haunted me for more than half a century: "It is necessary that we learn to love God without ever expecting that he will love us in return." Ethically, that has a certain poignance, but is it humanly acceptable? If you substitute Hamlet for God in Spinoza's observation, then I might understand it far better than I do. The popular Christian definition "God is love" fades away in the aura of Spinoza's inspired "intoxication," to use Coleridge's characterization of the great Jewish moralist as a "God-intoxicated man." If my reader is God-intoxicated, then she wisely will smile benignly enough at my qualms, but was Spinoza not talking about Yahweh and not Jesus Christ's God the Father? Spinoza's family, Iberian Marranos, had returned to Judaism in tolerant Amsterdam, where the synagogue, doubtless motivated by nervousness in regard to its Calvinist hosts, reluctantly excommunicated its best mind for his supposed "pantheism," in which Yahweh and his creation would not always be distinguished.

It makes little sense to say "Yahweh is love," or that we must love Yahweh. He just is not, never was, and never will be love. Many, if not most, of us at one time or another fall in love with someone who neither can accept love nor return it, though she or he perhaps demands it anyway, if only as worship or tribute. Until I Chronicles, Yahweh sets the pattern for such destructive role-playings, best exemplified in Shakespeare by Cleopatra—until Act V, when she apparently is transformed in the wake of Antony's death. Even there, Shakespeare endows her with an equivocal quality that is an endless challenge to actresses: how do you play the part of someone who no longer knows whether or not she is playing herself? When Yahweh, perhaps in love with David, as he may have been with Joseph, David's precursor, promises that he will be a father to Solomon, can we interpret the promise as other than divine dramatism?

I am aware that I am contravening the Sages of Judaism as well as the Christian theologians, but they possess in common a belated stance in regard to the Hebrew Bible, or Christian "Old" Testament. Yahweh necessarily is free of the Christian God the Father's anxiety of influence, and yet he exemplifies what Paul Valéry termed the influence of the poet's mind upon itself. The J Writer's Yahweh, who vitalizes parts of what we now call Genesis, Exodus, and Numbers, is nearly identical with the Lord God of II Samuel, and hovers like the Ghost of Hamlet's father in I Chronicles. Of all precursors, Yahweh is the strongest and least escapable.

Nietzsche warned against the tendency of the ancestor god to become a numinous shadow, a hint Freud took up (though he denied its derivation) in his marvelously mad *Totem and Taboo*, where the totem-father finally is slain by his sons, a horde of enemy brothers who cannibalize their dreaded forebear. This guilty act, according to Freud, is the origin of all religion and of culture. I am not grisly enough to suggest that those enemy brothers are the Gods of Judaism, Christianity, and Islam—that is, the very diverse fivefold of Adonai the Lord, God the Father, Jesus Christ, the Holy Spirit, and Allah. Freud's powerful speculation is, however, suggestive, in a Shakespearean way (as one should expect).

How much of Chronicles the great Redactor of "The Academy of Ezra" in Babylon composed, we cannot know, but certainly he arranged the Tanakh so that Chronicles concludes it. Weaving Yahweh into the palimpsest he created of the first three books of the Pentateuch, the Redactor (like Homer as much an author as an editor), attempted a revisionary softening of Yahweh, but that is like attempting to calm a whirlwind. Yahweh cannot be tamed. In Shakespearean terms, Yahweh fuses aspects of Lear, Falstaff, and Hamlet: Lear's unpredictable furies, Falstaff's surging vitalism, and Hamlet's restlessness of consciousness. Confronted by Yahweh's rhetorical questions, such as, will Leviathan and Behemoth make a covenant with you, either we abhor ourselves like Job, or we strike back vainly like Melville's Captain Ahab, most courageous and doom-eager of all Gnostics.

We know that, for many among us, Yahweh remains the most accurate answer to the anguished question "Who is God?" A Buddhist, Hindu, or Taoist would not agree, nor would many contemporary Christians, Muslims, and Jews, but mine is a literary critic's answer, and founds itself upon the force and power of the only literary personality that exceeds in vividness and memorability even Hamlet, Falstaff, Iago, Lear, Cleopatra. To transpose into religious terms, J's Yahweh is the most persuasive representation of transcendent *otherness* that I have ever encountered. And yet Yahweh is not only "anthropomorphic" (a hopeless term!) but absolutely human, and not at all a pleasant fellow, but then why should he be? He is not running for office, questing after fame, or seeking benign treatment in the media. If Christianity insists that Jesus Christ is the good news (an assertion that brutality by Christians throughout history has invalidated), then Yahweh is bad news incarnate, and Kabbalah tells us he most certainly has a body, an enormous one at that. It is an awful thing to fall into the hands of the living Yahweh.

I intend neither blasphemy nor irony here, but urge only some fresh perspectives. Loving Jesus is an American fashion, but loving Yahweh is a quixotic enterprise, misdirected because it refuses to know all the facts. You can respect Prospero and obey him, as everyone in *The Tempest* learns to do, but only Miranda loves him, since he has been both father and mother to her. In the Gospels (excluding John), Yahweh is the father of Jesus only as Abraham was Isaac's, on the single analogy of the Aqedah, the near sacrifice of the child as an offering to God.

14.

THE SON, O HOW UNLIKE

THE FATHER

NIETZSCHE, following Jakob Burckhardt, distinguished the
Hebrews' honoring of their fathers and mothers from the
Greeks' contest for the foremost place. Jesus reveres Yahweh as his father; the Qur'an has him deny to Allah that he ever sought equality
in the divine realm, let alone supremacy.

What is it to be like the Father? In *The God of Old* (2003), James Kugel
names a quality he calls "starkness," which resists precise definition
but comes down to the aura of Yahweh. Kugel's metaphor is profoundly evocative of the Psalms, with their emphasis upon our brief
life span in contrast with Yahweh's. Their answers to "What is man?"
tend to remind us of our smallness, though rarely with the stunning
voice of Yahweh out of the whirlwind at the end of the Book of Job.
Yahweh hears what Kugel terms "the cry of the victim," but starkness
renders his response more problematic than not. Kugel's God of Old
tends to stand behind the world, though sometimes he enters it.

Everything depends upon perceptiveness, both ours and that of the biblical writers.

Is Jesus Christ, like Yahweh, a God of this "starkness"? Christianity has insisted that Christ hears the cry of the victim and intercedes, when he can. By definition, Yahweh can, but all too often declines to intervene. The Christian populist Quaternity (Father, Son, Holy Ghost, Virgin Mother Mary) offers four potential intercessors, and actually many scores of others, angelic saints and saintly angels. Starkness hardly abides when such a crowd hears the cry of the victim. For Kugel, the Bible is now a lost world, but then I reaffirm the paradox I have invoked in previous books: Christianity (and Judaism) no longer are biblical religions, whatever their assertions. I am incapable of understanding what so many Christian scholars go on calling "the theology of the Old Testament." The Tanakh has *no* theology, and Yahweh, to keep repeating the obvious, is not at all a theological God. Theology was invented in Alexandria by the Hellenized Jew Philo, who interpreted the Septuagint as Plotinus construed Plato. Kugelian "starkness" happily is not theological, and doubtless approaches the perceptions of Scripture by Yeshua of Nazareth, and not at all by the Trinitarian Jesus Christ.

Yahweh disdains theologizing, but he is given to theophany, or self-manifestation. Unbounded, Yahweh still accepts a momentary series of dwindlings in order to show himself. Aside from warrior and storm appearances, these theophanies gravitate to the high places, hardly unique to Yahweh, but evidently particularly congenial to him and so in his possession, both at Sinai and on Zion, where Solomon built his Temple and where Isaiah beholds the enthroned God. Presumably the Temple throne is a representation of a grander, larger throne that Yahweh, on a more gigantic scale, occupies up above in his heavenly realms. Does Christianity expect us to envision the Christ as similarly enthroned, by the side of his Father? There are difficulties both aesthetic and spiritual in such a vision. I have mentioned previously that John Milton, perhaps too courageous in attempting to overcome these difficulties, gave us a Christ leading a Merkabah attack against Satan in *Paradise Lost,* a passage no one considers a poetic success. Nothing in the career of Jesus suggests a role as divine warrior.

(2)

Jews who continue to trust in the Covenant do not encounter the ambivalent Yahweh I describe, just as Christians who believe that Jesus was the Christ behold a very different figure from the one I regard. Perspective governs our response to everything we read, but most crucially with the Bible. Learning from scholars, whether Christian or Jewish, one still questions their conditioning, which too frequently overdetermines their presentation. Obviously that caution applies to me as well, a literary critic divided between Judaic heritage and a Gnostic discomfort with God.

James Kugel, like Kenneth Kuntz, nicely emphasizes that you don't find Yahweh in the Bible; he seeks *you* out. After all, his very name intimates that his presence depends upon his will. Though he seems to have been absent these last two millennia, Kugel rather grimly indicates that things were not much better for the Israelites when presumably Yahweh was on the job. Is it all, then, only a matter of perception, then as now? I like Donald Akenson's cheerful remark "I cannot believe that any sane person has ever liked Yahweh." But as Akenson adds, that is irrelevant, since Yahweh is reality. I would go a touch further and identify Yahweh with Freud's "reality-testing," which is akin to the Lucretian sense of the way things are. As the reality principle, Yahweh is irrefutable. We are all going to have to die, each in her or his turn, and I cannot agree with Jesus' Pharisaic belief in the resurrection of the body. Yahweh, like reality, has quite a nasty sense of humor, but bodily resurrection is not one of his Jewish or Freudian jokes.

(3)

The appeal of the Lord Jesus Christ cannot be in his perfectionism, where he goes beyond the Pharisees. Rather, he is made to offer a release from death's reality, from the way things are, and therefore also from Yahweh, who is replaced by a supposedly softened God the Father, both executioner and suicide, depending on precisely how you decide to interpret the Trinity. With no access to the historical Jesus, I am puzzled by my own split in receiving the literary character Jesus. The spiritual component in me responds to the at least proto-Gnostic Jesus of the Gospel of Thomas, while as a literary critic I am fascinated by the mysterious Gospel of Mark. Matthew does not find me, and Luke and Acts arouse only my skepticism, while John hates me and I respond in kind. Paul is utterly perplexing in my view, but stands aside anyway from whatever Jesus existed in history. D. H. Lawrence had a horror of the Revelation of John the Divine, which I share.

WHY DO MOST PEOPLE in the world, at all times and places, need God or the gods? Or, why does God need us? The questions are unanswerable or are answered too readily. Poets need gods because polytheism is poetry. Is Yahweh a poem? Is the Lord Jesus Christ? Christ either needs (or chooses) to love us, according to most Christians I encounter, and they choose (or need) to love him. A French Jewish philosopher has popularized a radical notion that some post-Holocaust Jews say their need is to love the Torah more than God. Yet all Kabbalah and much Talmud fuse Torah and Yahweh. Does Torah love us? I shrug off Yahweh when, for some moment or other, he affirms his love for the Jewish people. Palpably he doesn't, and *not* because we killed Christ; he did, using the Romans and a few Jewish Quislings as his agents. If Yahweh needed the Jews, or the Christians, or the Muslims, or the Zoroastrians, Hindus, Buddhists, Confucians, Taoists, and all the others, it appears he required feeding through sacrifices, and wanted also endless barrages of praise, prayers, hymns of gratitude, and immense love, unceasing love. Is Yahweh simply a cosmological and timeless King Lear, patriarch-of-patriarchs?

(4)

Sons and fathers can face off vexedly, in literature as in life. Freud judged *The Brothers Karamazov* supreme among novels, even as he rightly resented Dostoevsky's vicious anti-Semitism. One can see Prince Hal as a blend of Mitya and Ivan, with the role of old Karamazov divided between Henry IV and Falstaff. Certainly Dostoevsky gleaned hints from Shakespeare, just as Freud (with some bad faith) absorbed a good deal more from Shakespeare than from Dostoevsky. An Oedipal or Hamletian reading of Jesus in regard to his heavenly father is hardly innovative: that is what the Gnostic Jesus is all about, and is pithily expressed by William Blake, most vitalistic of all Gnostics: "The Son, O how unlike the Father."

The permanent puzzle of Yahweh is that we have no alternative to making sense of him in human terms, and yet he transcends any terms available to us. His moral character defies augury, and his personality is mercurial. The Jesus of Mark shares in this puzzle, as does Hamlet. To call the Tanakh's Yahweh a Shakespearean role gets things turned around: William Tyndale preceded Shakespeare, and I begin finally to understand that the English Bible, more even than Chaucer, though in fusion with the *Tales of Canterbury,* gave Shakespeare the precedent for his preternatural genius in creating women and men. That hardly intends to mean that Shakespeare was a Christian dramatist, though certainly he wrote for Christian audiences. Yahweh's being the prime model for Lear, and Mark's Jesus' being the same for Hamlet, do not mean the beliefs—whatever they were—of Shakespeare the man are on the stage. And yet so pervasive are the ironies of the J Writer that I cannot see how we are to determine the degree of trust (if any) that she had in the quicksilver Yahweh, a God upon whom absolutely you cannot rely.

Northern and Eastern gods can be tricksters, and perhaps all divinities, Yahweh included, ultimately had shamanistic origins, now frequently beyond trace. Yet another paradox is that Yahweh alternates between impish mischief and moral terror. Whoever initially wrote Mark kept this in mind: Yahweh both indulges and exploits what *we* would call his own narcissism. How could it be otherwise? Our memories of our mothers and fathers, if they have died, or our ongoing experiences of them, have many functions, but a key one is tempering our narcissism. Freud regards that as the formation of the above-I (superego) through internalization of the parents. Yahweh, shockingly human, has no parents, unlike the gods of the Greeks. Jack Miles, always challengingly on the point, wonders what keeps Yahweh going, since he has no precursors. Hamlet has the Ghost and Gertrude, and rejects Ophelia, who should have become his wife. How could we grasp Hamlet if the Ghost did not manifest, and if Gertrude and Ophelia were already dead?

As I read the play, Hamlet is incapable of loving anyone. Is Yahweh able to love? The Sages insist upon God's love of Israel, whatever her backslidings. Jesus, here at one with the Sages of Judaism, is convinced that his *abba* loves him, until at the end he cries out, "Father, why have you forsaken me?" I wish I could interpret the J text and Mark as stories of divine love, but I cannot, and keep asking myself, "Why not?" Yahweh is certainly the most impassioned of gods, zealous and jealous, but as I have noted, there is nothing in him like Lear's love for Cordelia, or Jacob's for Rachel. Love, Wittgenstein said, is not a feeling. Unlike pain, love is put to the test. One does not say, "That was not a true pain, because it passed away so quickly." By that test, Yahweh does not experience true love, whether for Israel or for all humankind. There are, as I keep admitting, as many versions of Jesus as there are people. The only two that impress me are incompatible with each other: the Gospels of Thomas and of Mark, which is not even compatible with itself. Gnostic Jesus teaches perception and not love;

Mark's Jesus cannot be said to love the disciples. If there is any real likeness between J's Yahweh and Mark's Jesus, it must be that both go on confounding our expectations. Can that be called love? Is a love you cannot live with pragmatically love? Shakespeare could not live with Anne Hathaway, though he went home to her in his final years. Yahweh could not marry, except metaphorically, and Jesus did not marry, a scandal in his tradition. Socrates loved neither his wife nor his disciples, and cannot be said to have loved Athens. Jesus wept over Jerusalem presumably out of love for his people.

(5)

The mass appeal, worldwide, of Christianity and of its rival, Islam, is founded upon simplicity of interpretation. Christianity's triumph over Judaism, in the early centuries of the Common Era, could not have come about on a theological basis. "Believe that Jesus was the Christ and you will be saved and live eternally" proved irresistible on the popular level. Later this was matched by "Submit to Allah on the authority of Muhammad, Seal of the Prophets, and you will be rewarded in the life to come." The survival of Yahwism could be for a remnant only. It was not any supposed distinction between Law and love that isolated Judaism, but an ongoing historical trauma. I expect no one to appreciate my surmise that holding on to Yahweh alone was and is to risk a perpetual trauma. Mark's Jesus, who anguished all night before his end, had been steadfast in devotion to Yahweh alone. If you argue that Jesus has saved countless others, it remains clear that himself he could not save.

15.

JESUS AND YAHWEH:
THE AGON FOR GENIUS

JACK MILES locates Yahweh as the would-be appropriator of all Jewish genius; hence the Circumcision becomes Yahweh's assertion that he alone is the fathering force. The other element of Greek *daemon* and Roman *genius* is thus omitted: all generation is divine, and there is no alter ego, until the Satan enters to commence the Book of Job. Jesus in the Gospels is the *mamzer,* or natural child, of Miriam, but directly engendered by Yahweh-as-Zeus, who thus first creates Jewish genius in Joshua of Nazareth. When Peter proclaims Jesus as Messiah, he is identified by Jesus as the apostle of alter ego: "Get thee behind me, Satan!" Jesus knows that his Yahweh-conferred genius is a death sentence, hardly to be evaded. There is no Blessing for Jesus as there was for the Patriarchs and for King David: the last in David's lineage will receive no earthly gift of more life into a time without boundaries. Only redemption *for others* awaits him.

IS JESUS, then, the resurgence of Jewish genius, pragmatically *against* Yahweh, even as it longs for Yahweh? Miles, in his *Christ,* gets around this agon by a total identification of Yahweh and Jesus, heavily reliant upon the Gospel of John and not upon Mark and Matthew. But that will not work, since Jesus and Yahweh are such different personalities: "The Son so unlike the Father!" All the subsequent theologies of the Incarnation refine St. John's but could not care less about personality. Joyce's Stephen Dedalus endorses the third-century African heretic Sabellius, "subtlest heresiarch of all the beasts of the field," who held that the Father was himself his own son, thus eliminating any anxiety of Yahweh's influence. Here I intend to develop the Sabellian heresy, particularly as regards the seizure by Jesus of Yahweh's daemonic, fathering force, the Sublime of Jewish genius.

Does it matter that Jesus and Yahweh are rather antithetical personalities, since Christian theology provides for a three-personed God, who nevertheless is of one substance? What substance, or which? Did Yahweh father himself, and if so, upon whom? The Catholic answer is very different from my questions, since the Virgin Birth has been a perpetually popular conceptual image, and Yahweh is not involved. It has always been a difficulty for Christian theology to unravel the precise relationship between Yahweh and the Holy Spirit. Can it indeed be only his breath that began creation by moving upon the face of the waters?

"Where shall wisdom be found?" the Book of Job's question, might be put to this matter also. Something in me always wishes to argue for a Gnostic Jesus, the Angel Christ, as Sufism termed him, who hovers flickeringly in John's Gospel. Such a Jesus can be found in the Gospel of Thomas, where crucifixion is totally irrelevant. Unfortunately, the canonical New Testament maintains historical priority over all extant Gnostic texts, the earliest of which are from the second century C.E. (except perhaps the Gospel of Thomas), and so revise Christian Scripture just as they do both the Tanakh and Plato, particularly his *Timaeus.* If there indeed were still earlier Gnostic texts, we have not found them. And yet we can hardly know what oral traditions were forever lost in the first-century Roman Holocaust of the Jews that culminated with the Temple's destruction in 70 C.E. Gershom Scholem, speaking with fierce authority, told me on several occasions that the Kabbalah of Merkabah and of the Divine Man Enoch/ Metatron had to have been orally transmitted secrets going back to at least the first century B.C.E. For this Milton of Kabbalistic studies, what he called the myth of Jesus was another product of those traditions.

Something is curiously absent from any history we possess of the Second Temple period, which covers almost three hundred years, from the Maccabean uprising against Syria to the Zealot rebellion against Rome, down to Bar Kochba and Akiba's last stand at Bethar against Hadrian, a tragic epilogue more than sixty years after the catastrophic end of the Temple. Jacob Neusner, unmatchable scholar of Judaistic origins, denies all scholarly myths of any early tradition that developed into "normative Judaism"—that is, what we now call Rabbinical, Talmudic Judaism. Merely as a literary critic, I have to observe that Neusner must be accurate. Religious scholars adore theology, but wherever Yahweh wills to be present, there can be no theology because, as I have argued throughout, absolutely Yahweh is not at all a concept. Yahweh in himself can be a dumbfoundering abyss, but there is almost as profound an abyss between Yeshua of Nazareth and Jesus-the-Christ—between "a marginal Jew," as Father Meier calls him, and a theological being who is both "true God" and "true Man" in Christian creeds. Yahweh and Jesus Christ remain separate though related puzzles. But what matters most about the God of the Tanakh is that he names himself Yahweh, since there was no one else who could have done it. Zeus usurps his own father, Chronos, but Yahweh is unfathered. Bereshith (Genesis) is not a beginning/again.

IF YOU HAVE HAD NO PARENTS, then no one has taught you; Yahweh necessarily is self-educated. Jesus has parents, and yet the New Testament has virtually no interest in Joseph, while its Mary (Miriam) is hardly the divinity exalted by the pope in 1950, when he belatedly proclaimed that the Mother of God was "assumed body and soul into heavenly glory" upon her earthly death. A century earlier, in 1854, she was accorded the Immaculate Conception, not the Virgin Birth (which had long been dogma) but the declaration that Mary's Mother also had been forever virginal. One skeptic in 1854 dared to wonder if Mary's maternal grandmother had retained *her* virginity, and yet the Church's theologians shrewdly understood when to stop.

I intend no irony by asking what could be made of the assertion that Mary was Yahweh's mother, since the Incarnation implies that Yahweh empties himself of his divinity and so dies as Jesus Christ upon the Cross. From a perspective that need not be regarded only as Jewish or Muslim, the pagan mystery aspect of Christianity is highlighted if you are willing to pursue the full consequences of Trinitarian doctrine. To say, with Tertullian, "I believe because it is absurd"

has a period flavor. Is the Crucifixion more Theater of the Absurd
than it is tragic drama?

(2)

Father Meier has preceded me in meditating upon Jesus as an instance
of "Jewish genius." Yahweh is Jewish genius itself—an unstable genius, yet so is the Jesus of Mark, who is restlessly rapid and incessantly
moves through crowds. When Americans say "Jesus helps" and "Jesus
saves," they unknowingly rely upon the root meaning of the name
Joshua (Yeshua), which is "Yahweh helps" or "Yahweh saves." Do Jesus and Yahweh help and save in similar ways? In the Book of Joshua,
when Yahweh is a swordsman commanding the Israelite warriors,
this aid leads to the salvation of the conquest. John Milton, in *Paradise
Lost,* baroquely extends this tradition when his Christ leads an ar-
mored attack upon Satanic rebels, driving them into the abyss so that
their flaming impact on the bottom creates Hell. That is thoroughly
Yahwistic but hardly consonant with the Jesus Christ of the Gospels.
As I have mentioned, Milton, a radical Protestant sect of one (unless
you agree with Christopher Hill that the poet was a Muggletonian),
gets Jesus off the Cross with startling haste, because he refuses to accept a self-immolated Yahweh.

I repeat that the future of Christianity is not in Europe or the Middle East, but in the United States, Africa, and Asia. This coming Christianity is dominated by Jesus and the Holy Spirit, rather than by the
figure of the Father. A pragmatic separation between Yahweh and Jesus widens, and Yahweh has not survived in Christianity, but only in

the Allah of Islam. The dying God has also turned out to be Yahweh, and not Jesus.

All gods age, Yahweh included, though *his* dying may not prove to be final, since Islam could yet prevail. Gods ebb with continental economies, and Europe's augmenting godlessness could be a symptom of its final decline in relation to globalization. The Jesus Christ of evangelical Protestantism and of Mormonism is the not-so-hidden God of the corporate world in the United States.

Why was Christianity triumphant from its adoption by the murderous Emperor Constantine until its gradual intellectual displacement since the Enlightenment? If you are a believing Christian, there is no problem: the truth has made you free. That is also Islam's answer. Cultures rise and ebb; Gibbon ironically viewed the fall of the Roman Empire as Christianity's fault. Since the American Empire is only ostensibly Christian, our eventual decline and fall will have to be ascribed to some different culprit. Chinese and Indians work harder than we do, while Europeans increasingly evade labor. Norwegians, French, and many other nationalities notoriously embrace absenteeism. Was Christianity's concealed persistence a kind of work ethic, inherited from the hard existence of Judea? We still identify capitalism with Protestantism, and Puritan ideas pervade our market economy. Business leadership in the United States is an oddly pragmatic blend of American Jesus and Machiavelli.

Agon, the ancient Greek contest for the foremost place, was contrasted by Nietzsche to the Hebrews' honoring of their fathers and mothers, the placing of their forerunners before themselves. In the agon between Jesus-the-Christ and Yahweh, the struggle is concealed by dimming Yahweh's sublimity into the flickering candlelight of

God the Father. When the Gospel of John's Jesus is made to say, "Before Abraham was, I am," should we interpret this to mean that he also will be present only when he chooses to be? In Isaiah, as throughout the Tanakh, Yahweh's presence does not become an absence even when Yahweh eclipses himself. Jack Miles, in his lively *God: A Biography,* argues that Yahweh pulls back into heaven after the Book of Job. This withdrawal accounts for the characteristic anxiety that marks the Hebrew narrative; the Tanakh's question always is "Will Yahweh act?" The ultimate answer implied is that he will not, and has deserted us, perhaps because he is caught up in the contradictions of his own character and personality. The Sages of the Talmud would not agree with such an interpretation, and yet post-Holocaust Jewry is confronted by this enigma. The Roman Holocaust of the Jews, with its first climax at the fall of Jerusalem and destruction of Yahweh's Temple, and a second one after the even larger-scale devastation of the Bar Kochba rebellion, resulted in the rise and persistence of Rabbinical Judaism. A remnant of that faith still struggles on, yet many of its adherents avert themselves from asking, Is it possible still to trust in a Covenant that Yahweh pragmatically has forsaken? If you have lost your grandparents in the German death camps, are you to trust a Yahweh who must be either powerless or uncaring? Jewish Gnosticism, in my judgment, took its inception from the initial Roman Holocaust.

(3)

Once again, what do Christians mean when they say that God is love? Secularists ironically reverse this into the hazardous view that love is

God. I do not know anyone who loves her enemies and who prays for those who persecute her. St. Paul says that Christ was the son of Yahweh's love, while the Gospel of John frequently insists that to not love God is to not know him, an exhortation which has become creedal.

And yet Paul and John established the path by which Christian theology arrived at the doctrine of the impassability of the Father: his freedom from, or inability to feel, human emotion. That is Plato's God and not Yahweh the jealous (or zealous) God of the Hebrews. Plato, by the time he conceptualized his theology, had aged beyond his earlier exaltation of Socratic *eros.* Socrates does not appear in the *Laws.* An apathetic God cannot be identified with love. The great theologian Origen, seeking the perfection of a sexless God, is said by Eusebius to have castrated himself. Gnosticism, condemned by the Church as heresy, preached the impassability of Christ, who thus did not suffer, even upon the Cross. There was therefore no Passion.

Origen and the Gnostics were more consistent than were the Christians, who affirmed that God was love and still totally transcendent, even as the Creator. How can what is so far beyond us also love us? The Christian answer has to be the Atonement, in which the embodiment of God's love for the world and its people accepts sacrifice as the only mode of reconciling God with them, and so forgiving them for every sin, Adam's onward. Augustine, in consequence, could restore the idea of God as love by seeing God as he who loves, his Son as the beloved, and the Holy Spirit as the love the Father and the Son share. That formulation is more than ingenious, though it engenders fresh puzzles.

(4)

My favorite observation in Spinoza I have cited before: it is necessary that we learn to love God without expecting that he ever will love us in return. An unrequited love can be an imaginative benefit to poets, but not to most of us. Spinoza, though cast out by his fellow Jews in Amsterdam, was intoxicated with Yahweh rather than with the Christian God the Father. Love and the fear of Yahweh are one; I cannot recall the New Testament speaking of the fear of God the Father. The Yahwist's God did not *create* out of love, though his motive was to make a human in his own image. Moses (Deuteronomy 6:5) commands the Hebrews to love God with all their heart, soul, and might but he does not say the love will be reciprocated; and the Sages said that "reverence" is what Moses means by loving God, since the context of this love is the Covenant. This is not to fall into the rhetoric of the Christian misconception of the "Old" Covenant in which Yahweh is William Blake's Nobodaddy. The Christian God the Father supposedly can be loved without fear, but in fully human as in spiritual actuality there is always a fusion of love and fear, even between equals.

Yahweh is a personality without a sexual component. For Sigmund Freud, that was no problem, since he cheerfully referred to himself as a "godless Jew." I myself find Freud's phrase an oxymoron; Yahweh is hard to just dismiss. But then, Freud was nevertheless at his least persuasive in *The Future of an Illusion*. Yahweh, called Allah by Islam, is a very dangerous "illusion" these days, and so is as much a reality as ever before. Like Yahweh, Allah in the Qur'an is perpetually furious with us—a tightly regimented fury. Yahweh's Covenant with Israel demands a reverent or loyal love, and offers a kind of love in return, one difficult to describe, since it cannot be distinguished from compassion. If a person is told one loves her, and she replies, "I feel compassion for you," that is not what most of us want from another. It is rather too godlike, and who would accept it, except from God?

Christianity reads the Suffering Servant passage in II Isaiah (52:13–53:12) as a prophecy of the Crucifixion. The Sages of the Oral Law shrugged this off, some suggesting that the Suffering Servant was Moses and others that it was also Jeremiah the prophet, in fusion with the people of Israel. There is a useful study of the influence of Jeremiah and of I Isaiah upon II Isaiah, *A Prophet Reads Scripture,* by Benjamin D. Sommer (1998). That the Suffering Servant "accepts his fate more readily than Jeremiah" (Sommer, 66) does not lessen the later prophet's deliberate reliance upon the earlier, as on I Isaiah, who is part of the fused Servant figure of Suffering Israel, as again Sommer shows. The Gospels, which declare the crucified and risen Jesus the fulfillment of Israel's prophetic tradition, have a far more anxious relationship to Jeremiah and both Isaiahs, and Zechariah also, than the Hebrew prophets have to one another.

Does divine love take on a new dimension when Yahweh incants the major Suffering Servant song? No rabbinical sage or modern Jewish scholar of the Bible would wish to say so, yet that pragmatically abandons the matter to Christianity's strong misreading of this extraordinary poem:

> "Indeed, My servant shall prosper,
> Be exalted and raised to great heights.
> Just as the many were appalled at him—
> So marred was his appearance, unlike that of man,

His form, beyond human semblance—

Just so he shall startle many nations.

Kings shall be silenced because of him,

For they shall see what has not been told them,

Shall behold what they never have heard."

"Who can believe what he have heard?

Upon whom has the arm of the Lord been revealed?

For he has grown, by His favor, like a tree crown,

Like a tree trunk out of arid ground.

He had no form or beauty, that we should look at him:

No charm, that we should find him pleasing.

He was despised, shunned by men,

A man of suffering, familiar with disease.

As one who hid his face from us,

He was despised, we held him of no account.

Yet it was our sickness that he was bearing,

Our suffering that he endured.

We accounted him plagued,

Smitten and afflicted by God;

But he was wounded because of our sins,

He bore the chastisement that made us whole,

And by his bruises we were healed.

We all went astray like sheep,

Each going his own way;

And the Lord visited upon him

The guilt of all of us."

He was maltreated, yet he was submissive,

He did not open his mouth;

Like a sheep being led to slaughter,

Like a ewe, dumb before those who shear her,

He did not open his mouth.

By oppressive judgment he was taken away,

Who could describe his abode?

For he was cut off from the land of the living

Through the sin of my people, who deserved the punishment.

And his grave was set among the wicked,

And with the rich, in his death—

Though he had done no injustice

And had spoken no falsehood.

But the Lord chose to crush him by disease,

That, if he made himself an offering for guilt,

He might see offspring and have long life,

And that through him the Lord's purpose might prosper.

Out of his anguish he shall see it;

He shall enjoy it to the full through his devotion.

"My righteous servant makes the many righteous,

It is their punishment that he bears;

Assuredly, I will give him the many as his portion,

He shall receive the multitude as his spoil.

For he exposed himself to death

And was numbered among the sinners,

Whereas he bore the guilt of the many

And made intercession for sinners."

A resonance is vibrant here that gives Yahweh an unique tonality, anticipated in Jeremiah and I Isaiah but not with this precise pathos.

The German-Jewish philosopher Franz Rosenzweig, who died in early middle age in 1929, argued that God must fall in love with his creation. I do not find in the Tanakh any indication that this happened, but the genius who composed II Isaiah shows us Yahweh, confronted by the Suffering Servant, falling in love with the tormented people of Israel. What is shockingly powerful about this major Suffering Servant passage is that it *is* a kind of divine love song. To make such an observation is very uncomfortable to me, for reasons both historical and personal. But it is for me a burden that Christianity's usurpation of this astonishing poem is imaginatively difficult to dispute, though also unacceptable from any Jewish perspective.

Indebted as he was to his precursors, II Isaiah is a strong prophet-poet, frighteningly original in his metaphor of the Suffering Servant. It is important to keep noting that the Servant is *not* a Messianic figure in the Hebrew text. II Isaiah celebrates King Cyrus of Persia, quite explicitly, as the Messiah, because the prophet's purpose is to persuade the comfortable Israelites of Babylon to abandon their Exile and return to Jerusalem, a freedom proclaimed for them by Cyrus the Messiah. The Babylonian Diaspora can be thought of as startlingly like the current condition of American Jewry, which is not ever going to go back to Zion. II Isaiah does not seem to have persuaded most of those at ease in Babylon to choose an arduous existence in Jerusalem.

The Suffering Servant is a plural being, the people of Israel, both men and women, and their stricken prophet Jeremiah. If the great chant is a song of love, this is a love difficult to distinguish from death. Walt Whitman's songs that fuse love and death are clear analogues. The forlorn male seabird of "Out of the Cradle Endlessly Rocking" and the solitary hermit thrush of "When Lilacs Last in the Dooryard

Bloom'd" are curiously akin in their love songs of death to Yahweh's compassionate lament for his Suffering Servant, Israel. Perhaps you need to be a believing Christian to call Yahweh's chant an unequivocal expression of his love.

Kabbalah turns Yahweh into Ein-Sof, "without end," and audaciously charts his sexual life with his beloved Shekhinah, the female indwelling presence of Yahweh among us. The Kabbalistic baroque elaborations of the Shekhinah relied for their starting point upon the copious (but chaste) musings of the Sages in the two Talmuds and the midrashim. There is an illuminating introduction to the Talmudic Shekhinah in Ephraim E. Urbach's *The Sages* (pp. 37–65). Urbach emphasizes that for the great rabbis the Shekhinah had no separate existence of her own but was a part of God, his presence in the world. But this changed in the eleventh century, when the Shekhinah begins to be spoken of as female and as having her own existence. Her extraordinary flowering in Kabbalah assimilated the Shekhinah to the Lady Wisdom of Proverbs 8:22–9:6.

In the Prophets, the Shekhinah is never a protagonist, and it took the ingenuities of Kabbalah to associate her with any prophetic context. The Suffering Servant is all Israel, both men and women, and whatever compassion or loving-kindness the Servant evokes in Yahweh is not easy to define, and yet is central to the difference between his fatherly stance toward Israel and the Trinity's God the Father's stance toward his Son, Jesus-the-Christ. I repeat that the Servant *cannot* be the anointed one, the Messiah, but must be the crying-out victim that Cyrus, as Yahweh's Messiah, is coming to save.

16.

THE JEWISH SAGES
ON GOD

YAHWEH, as a profoundly human God, does not yield fruitfully to theology, a Greek and not a Hebrew mode of thinking. As I have noted, the nature of the Christian God the Father is radically different from Yahweh's personality and character. Theology does not ascribe personality to God the Father, to Jesus Christ the Son, or to the Holy Spirit. When the Kabbalists renamed Yahweh (his name a taboo), they called him Ein-Sof, "without end." And so he was, and is, wherever one now thinks he is.

The God of the Gnostics is called the Stranger or Alien God, and has exiled himself from our cosmos, perhaps forever. I do not regard Yahweh in that way, but he perhaps last appears in the Tanakh as the rather remote Ancient of Days of the Book of Daniel (about 164 B.C.E.). The text is the Aramaic Chapter 7, in which various Gentile tyrannies manifest as terrible beasts from the sea, and then in Verses 9–10 we see this:

As I looked on,

Thrones were set in place,

And the Ancient of Days took His seat.

His garment was like white snow,

And the hair of His head was like lamb's wool.

His throne was tongues of flame;

Its wheels were blazing fire.

A river of fire streamed forth before Him;

Thousands upon thousands served Him;

Myriads upon myriads attended Him;

The court sat and the books were opened.

That is aesthetically impressive, but not very Yahwistic, since this is presumably God sitting as the president or king of a heavenly court, as in Isaiah or Job. Jack Miles, exuberantly shrewd, thinks Yahweh has become a silent old man, soon to subside into utter weariness. As an anxious student of Yahweh, I am skeptical, and remember that the Book of Daniel is rather different in the context of the Christian Testament than in the Tanakh. For Christians, Daniel is a major prophet, akin to Isaiah, Jeremiah, and Ezekiel, which is an absurd inflation. For Jews, Daniel is not even a minor prophet, and is placed in the Kethuvim, or Writings, in between Esther and Ezra. The Dead Sea Covenanters at Qumran regarded Daniel as a prophet, but as apocalyptics they recognized one of their own.

The J Writer and other authors of saga were not apocalyptics, and Yahweh is unhappy with that mode. He walks about on earth, as befits a meddler. The Sages of the Jewish people were severely challenged to accommodate themselves to their unnerving God, but they magnificently confronted their task most notably in the Mishnah and in the Babylonian Talmud, two amazing works. The Mishnah codifies the Oral Law upon which Rabbinical Judaism is founded, and is traditionally credited to "Rabbi" himself, Judah the Patriarch (about 200 C.E.). Bavli (the Babylonian Talmud) studies all Torah, written and oral, and really cannot be dated. It may have been concluded anytime from 520 to 600 C.E., and makes for considerably attractive reading and study, in contrast to the forbidding Mishnah, an indubitably great work that depresses me. As Donald Harman Akenson remarks, the Mishnah is both Hermetic and "perfect," a perfection I find destructive. In contrast, Bavli is an open splendor, inviting a lifetime's education, but only on its own stringent terms.

I CANNOT RECALL that the Hebrew Bible ever explicitly states that the Jewish people can render themselves holy through study, yet I am one of many thousands who were brought up to believe in such incessant reading and meditation. The idea now seems to me Platonic, and reached the rabbis both of Jerusalem and Babylon through Hellenism. It is a puzzle that so many of the Jewish Sages of the first through sixth centuries C.E. could trust in Yahweh's Covenant despite reading the Tanakh through Platonic lenses, as it were. Their Yahweh remained a human god, frequently to their consternation, as they struggled to explain away divine "anthropomorphism"—a word that, as I keep mentioning, I dislike and reject in this context. The greatest Jewish sages recognized quite thoroughly that it was better to see the Patriarchs as "theomorphic" men than to view Yahweh as an "anthropomorphic" god. But divest Yahweh of his human propensities and attributes, and you may as well adopt the God of Platonic theology. Despite Philo of Alexandria, prince of Jewish Platonic allegorists, a true name for God, in the tradition of Rabbi Akiba, is Ish (man). Exodus 15:3 magnificently intones, "Yahweh is a Man of War, the Lord is his name." Yahweh reveals himself to the embattled legions of Joshua, Moses' general, as a man in order to sanctify and to strengthen an Israel embattled then, through the ages, right now, and doubtless forever to come, since all the road maps are illusory traps that offer only suicide to the State of Israel. One reflects that even such suicide would not appease the rapaciousness of French and other European anti-Semitism, which contrives to survive even the ebbing-away of European Christianity.

THE GREAT AKIBA, who truly founded the Judaism we still recognize (even when we can neither accept nor reject it, my own dilemma), held strong to the literalism of Yahweh as Ish, God as Man, despite Rabbi Ishmael and his school. Yahweh walks about in Exodus 13:21, however unhappy such perambulation was to make the Prophets. I find a crazy comedy in the early exegetes who follow a strolling Yahweh around, while chirping, "He's not walking!" After all, the hardworking and energetic Yahweh really *rests* on the seventh day, doubtless loafing and inviting his soul, rather in Walt Whitman's manner. A swordsman, Yahweh needs downtime, like all men of war. And Yahweh is joyous, or angry, and frequently hungry. Akiba sensibly found all this quite acceptable, but it roused his friend and opponent Ishmael to indignant denials that God and the Angels required sustenance, even though the picnics at Mamre and on Sinai plainly affirm Yahweh's appetite.

For most Western people, God is either personal or does not matter. The Neoplatonic One may have a handful of scholarly adherents worldwide, but not more. Catholics pray to Jesus and the Blessed Virgin Mother, but rarely to God the Father or the Holy Spirit. American Religionists, whether ostensibly Protestant or Catholic, talk to Jesus or, if Pentecostalists, are imbued with the Holy Spirit. Yahweh, under other names, is still prayed to by Jews, and under the name of Allah by Muslims. God for all these has to understand and even share many human feelings, or he would shrink away to irrelevance.

Philo of Alexandria, even if he was the mystic that Erwin R. Goodenough described him as being, was scandalized by the human Yahweh of the Tanakh. That helps explain why Philo was ignored by Rabbinical Judaism, and survived pragmatically only as a theologian weirdly adopted by Christianity. What were the Jews to do with Philo's assertion that Yahweh "is not susceptible of any passion at all"?

Akiba's Yahwistic literalism remains refreshing today, since it helped preserve God's extraordinary personality (not to mention Akiba's own). What we call Judaism today, in any of its varieties, essentially remains the religion of Akiba, who is the dominant personality (another word won't do) in the Mishnah, and the master of the superb Sages (Judah ben Ilai and Meir particularly) most often cited there. Despite some recent scholarship, I find no reason to doubt the historical tradition that the aged Akiba (40–135 c.e.) was horribly martyred by the Roman Emperor Hadrian, after the defeat of the heroic Simon Bar Koziva, whom Akiba had proclaimed the Messiah, and renamed

Bar Kochba ("son of a star," see Numbers 24:17). The Bar Kochba Rebellion (132–35 C.E.) was on an enormous scale, dwarfing even the disaster of the Jewish War and destruction of the Temple, and Akiba's Yahwistic literalism was carried through into martyrdom.

THE AKIBAN LITERALISM has a curious monument in the famous *Shi'ur Komah*, brilliantly analyzed by Gershom Scholem in the title essay of *On the Mystical Shape of the Godhead* (1991). Though we have no manuscripts of *Shi'ur Komah* earlier than the eleventh century, oral tradition assigns this astonishing booklet to Akiba himself, nine hundred years earlier, and it certainly accords with his teaching. *Shi'ur Komah* means something like "The Measure of the Body," which here shockingly is Yahweh's own. Whenever they were composed, they are grotesque, as their Yahweh is gigantic, a cosmic giant in height, length of limbs, facial features, and stride. Akiba was particularly devoted to Solomon's Song of Songs, canonized only through the heroic rabbi's insistence, and the Song of Songs is clumsily imitated in *Shi'ur Komah,* which is merely a heap of esoteric fragments, rather than a sublimely ordered suite of extraordinary love poems. It is in the *Zohar,* the central work of all Kabbalah, composed by Moses de Leon and his circle in medieval Spain, that the crude suggestions of *Shi'ur Komah* undergo extraordinary elaborations.

(2)

Creation, according to the Sages, has the simple object of the human: Yahweh had no other purpose. And Yahweh was monistic in his approach: Hebrew Man does not divide into flesh against spirit, but is "a living soul." Pauline dualism, which eventually ensues in the Cartesian separation of mind and body, is Platonic and not Judaic. Presumably the Christian God-the-Father does not, like Yahweh, have a body, except in Mormonism. I can recall no text in which God-the-Father emulates Yahweh's picnics at Mamre and on Sinai. I see little difference between Plato's God, in *The Laws,* and Christianity's divinity, and even less between Aristotle's Unmoved Mover and the supposed Father of Jesus Christ, though Aristotle's God couldn't care less about us, and the Christian deity sacrifices his Son so as to save us. A person without a personality would be an impossible description of Yahweh, but it does well enough for the First Person of the Trinity. St. Augustine's God is not at all distant from that of Plotinus, who modified Plato's theology into a doctrine of the World-Soul. Plato urged us "to pry the soul loose and isolate it from the body." Plotinus and Augustine were glad to obey; the Rabbinical Sages were not.

Any religion that totally expunges the "anthropomorphic" also turns away from Yahweh, who is a *man* of war, and of much besides. Rabbi Akiba, as we have seen, insisted that God was literally Ish, a man. The human aspect of Jesus, as "true man," is reconcilable with that, but the "true god" is not, since such a God was more that of Plato than of Moses.

17.

SELF-EXILE OF YAHWEH

S O ENIGMATIC IS YAHWEH that his creation of man, woman, and the world can be viewed as self-exile. This idea is not my own, but is Kabbalistic, and may go back to earlier Gnostic speculations about a crisis in the inner life of the creator, a crisis I will describe in this chapter. The mythic act called *zimzum*—divine self-exile—is mentioned in medieval Kabbalistic texts, and then achieves centrality in the sixteenth-century master of Kabbalah, Isaac Luria, who during his sojourn in Safed, in Turkish-ruled northern Palestine, taught a Gnostic Kabbalah, which ever since has been vastly influential. Shaul Magid in *Beginning/Again* (2002) argues that *zimzum*, which is a metaphor for Yahweh's "contraction" or "withdrawal" from part of himself in order to inaugurate creation, is a myth about Yahweh's own origins.

The mystery of Yahweh is in his self-naming as a presence who can also choose to be absent. Both the glories and the catastrophes of Jewish history imply a God who exiles himself by withdrawing from his commitment to the Covenant. Is this withdrawal the ultimate cost of creation? Talmudic commentary never (so far as I know) meditates upon Yahweh *before* his act of creation; that freed Kabbalah for its own speculations.

Zimzum is related to a verb meaning "to sharply draw in the breath." Yahweh had breathing trouble and thus inaugurated our cosmos. Kafka remarked that we were one of God's thoughts on one of his bad days. Try holding your breath in as long as you can: if you can think at all, there will be difficulty in sustaining such thought.

Few other moments in literature are as memorable as Yahweh's opening act in Genesis 2:4–7, the work of the J Writer, rather than the Priestly Creation in Genesis 1 to 2:3. We are not in Babylonia five centuries later, but probably in Solomon's reign, about a thousand years before the Common Era:

> When Yahweh made earth and heaven—when no shrub of the field was yet on earth and no grasses of the field had yet sprouted, because Yahweh had not sent rain upon the earth and there was no man to till the soil, but a flow would well up from the ground and water the whole surface of the earth—Yahweh formed man from the dust of the earth. He blew into his nostrils the breath of life, and man became a living being.

How deliberate is a forming of Adam from the *adamah,* or dusty red clay? The description above is rather like that of a child shaping a mud figurine and then magically breathing life into it. We have to surmise Yahweh's motives for so expanding a playfulness as to have made a cosmos to accommodate his Adam. By doing so, God accepts self-limitation: the world he has created is a reality separate from him. One can regard this separateness as augmentation rather than diminishment, but soon enough Yahweh experiences anxiety at what he has done. II Samuel, contemporary with the Yahwist (if not indeed also by her), tells us that God granted the angels the consciousness of knowing both good and evil. Somehow the serpent has gained this knowledge, which helped aid Christian misinterpretation of him as a fallen angel. But there is no "somehow" in Yahweh's outburst of anxiety that Adam blindly might eat of the Tree of Life and thus become one of the Elohim, or angels. For the first time we are made aware of the violent unpredictability of Yahweh.

By creating the human, Yahweh either has become more human himself, or undesignedly has revealed that he already was all too human. *Zimzum* is an enabling act, in which God paradoxically multiplies by contraction. We are not told why or if Yahweh accepts self-curtailment, though from the start he manifests ambivalence toward his creatures. It is the peculiar strength of Kabbalah that it ventures where Talmud and philosophical theology did not care to trespass, the ambiguous doubleness in Yahweh's personality, in which he both wants us to be and is bothered by our existence. Exegesis that avoids esotericism also evades the puzzles of divine creativity.

The Tanakh gives us no account of Yahweh's origin. He has no father and no mother and seems to tumble out of the pages of a book he may have written. Perhaps he wrote before he spoke, and had to fashion an audience to read and to hear him. Should that be his elusive motive for risking creation, then he would differ only in degree, not in kind, from any author I know.

There has to be a less narcissistic purpose in God's impulse, though I am haunted by Freud's ironic remark that it is necessary to fall in love lest the ego choke upon its own self-delight. But as I have remarked earlier, Yahweh, even if he becomes infatuated with King David, cannot be said to manifest more than Covenant-love for the people of Israel, when they are sufficiently loyal vassals to his overlordship. His Othello-like fury of jealousy provoked by Israel's whoring after strange gods is considerably surpassed by his Lear-like stormy rages against the people's ingratitude. Still the question remains: Why did he ever jeopardize his mysterious freedom by blundering into the self-exile of creation?

Kabbalah matters because it audaciously attempts several mysterious answers to this question of origins. Most profoundly, the later, or "regressive," Kabbalah of Isaac Luria reopens Yahweh to his sufferings and our own. According to this tradition, there is a sexual life (Freud would say "drive") *within* Yahweh, most deftly interpreted in Moshe Idel's *Kabbalah and Eros* (2005). To the life-drive, Freud juxtaposes his death-drive, the radical speculation that animates his weirdly elegant *Beyond the Pleasure Principle* (1919). It delights me that during his labor on this book, Freud briefly entertained the alarming idea that the death-drive was fueled by *destrudo,* a negative energy, in order to complement libido in the vital order. Fortunately, the Great Conquistador (as he liked to term himself) dropped *destrudo* as being a touch too dualistic. Otherwise we would all go about and lie down murmuring about this entropic rocket fuel even as we are persuaded we possess libido, a separate sexual energy, which in fact does not exist.

Even if, as either good or bad Freudians (we have no other options), we bestow libido upon Yahweh, we have not gone a long way into accounting for his motive in making (and botching) the creation. *Zimzum* is a glorious metaphor for God's travail in breaking the vessels that he had contrived to receive his dangerous light but that failed to contain his creative exuberance. It is in that exuberance, Yahweh's extravagance of sheer being, that Lurianic Kabbalah subtly locates the subversive gnosis that, for some of us, partly illuminates the visible darkness of the Hebrew God.

In the Elder Edda of the Northern mythology, the high god Odin hangs upon Yggdrasil, the World Tree, nine days and nights, in order to gain knowledge of the runes. He hopes thus (vainly) to avert the twilight of the gods, which the runes foretell. Does Yahweh possess full knowledge of the future? Can anyone, if he remembers no past? Yahweh defies foregrounding. His early history has been chronicled by the J Writer; the challenge is God's prehistory. Kierkegaard's Nebuchadnezzar, restored to human status after eating grass like an ox, asks who taught Yahweh his wisdom? But Yahweh, before the Proverbs ascribed to Solomon, hardly was a wise God.

Isaac Luria's fable of *zimzum* and *shevirat ha-kelim,* the Breaking of the Vessels, hints at Yahweh's secret—that in order to create, God had to cut himself down. The triple rhythm of self-exile, breaking of primordial vessels, and subsequent *tikkun* (restoration or redemption) defines the inner life of God, and is unlikely to have begun with Genesis. To ask what is the origin of origin seems absurd, yet why do we find coherence in the Death of God, whether in the Nietzschean or the Christian sense, and not in the birth of Yahweh? Christians revere the birth of Jesus the Christ-child, and the descent of the Holy Spirit, but no theologian wonders about the origin of the Holy Father.

Whether the strong light of the canonical Hebrew Bible and its mirror of Yahweh's will constitute a perfection that destroys (Gershom Scholem) or absorbs (Moshe Idel), either way the Kabbalah exists to receive that light. Reception itself is a further breaking-apart of the vessels—and so alters creation, by ruining earlier worlds. Not a Kabbalist, I seek in Luria's dialectic of creation what the strong poets sought and found in Plato, that professed enemy of Homer. Call it an uncertain path to transcendence, or following in the wake of Yahweh's self-exile.

LURIA BEGINS HIS DOCTRINE of creation by reversing the Neoplatonic myth of emanation common to all of Kabbalah he had inherited. Yahweh is too holy a name for the Kabbalists, as it was for the Talmudic Sages, who called him Adonai (for the most part). The Kabbalists, though, named him Ein-Sof ("without end"), emphasizing his infinite and hidden nature. Before Luria's revelations in Safed, Ein-Sof created by emanating outward into the world as he made it. But in a massive and daring turn, Luria centered upon the inner life of God.

Luria did not invent *zimzum;* he took it from his teacher, Moses Cordovero of Safed, who himself had received it from tradition, both Talmudic and Kabbalistic. But Luria extraordinarily reinvented it, even as Shakespeare inherited the human, inner self from Ovid and Chaucer, and Tyndale's Protestant biblical translations, and then remolded it. We never will know if Shakespeare, like his father, was a recusant Catholic, but his dependence on the Protestant Bible makes me guess otherwise. Isaac Luria, the sacred Lion of his people, was a mystic saint and no rebel, yet he must have been aware of the subversive potential of his recasting of *zimzum* from a Neoplatonized rabbinical trope to a Gnostic opening-up of an abyss within Yahweh, a void akin to our own aching sense of emptiness and suffering.

All Jewish exegesis, from Hillel and Yeshua of Nazareth through the two Talmuds and Kabbalah on through Judah Halevi's *Kuzari* and Maimonides, and perhaps culminating in Kafka and Freud, can be termed a series of endeavors to open the Tanakh to the historical sufferings of the people Yahweh chose as his own. *Zimzum,* as the process can be interpreted, seems to suggest that Jewish suffering begins within Yahweh himself, in his acts of creation. The original term, in all rabbinical usage, means that God has to fall into himself (as it were) in order to get creation started. Luria located the catastrophe-creation in the Breaking of the Vessels, which could not sustain the rigor of the outpouring of Yahweh's strict light of judgment. But that was *our* catastrophe; the *zimzum* was God's.

IN THE CAMPAIGN OF CREATION, Yahweh commences by *re-treating.* Perhaps the Divine Warrior, wily in his struggle against the forces of chaos, made a strategic withdrawal. Luria is endlessly subtle, but so was the Old Rabbinic Doctrine of God. Lawrence Fine, in his very useful *Physician of the Soul, Healer of the Cosmos* (2003), traces the path of Scholem and of Idel in backgrounding Luria's own sources. In one rabbinical midrash, on Exodus 25:8–10, Yahweh curtails himself, really concentrates into scarcely a presence, in order to fit into the portable ark of the Covenant. Is there a pragmatic difference between this Jane Austen–like dwindling into a wifely role and Isaac Luria's pulling-back of God? Scholem insisted there was, but is this a difference that makes a difference?

In Freudian terms, as I once suggested to Scholem, pre-Kabbalistic *zimzum* can seem rather like the dismal comedy of Yahweh's superego punishing the divine ego, a notion the majestic Scholem scornfully dismissed. Freud, Kafka wrote, was the Rashi of contemporary Jewish anxieties, a jest that Scholem gleefully enjoyed quoting to me. Fine shrewdly points to other midrashim, where God contracts himself into the Holy of Holies in the Jerusalem Temple. Ein-Sof means "without limits," but every act of all-too-human Yahweh involves accepting a further limitation.

Gnosticism, Jewish and Gentile, spoke of divine degradation, of a rift opening within the demiurgic cosmocrator. The Gnostic rebellion, literary to the heart of its darkness, compounded Plato's *Timaeus* with Genesis, an ironically bitter fusion that Hans Jonas termed the "intoxication of unprecedentedness," truly an imaginative making-it-new. Scholem and Idel, in contrary ways, suggest that Gnosticism was merely a belated repetition of archaic Judaistic speculations, and indeed pre-Kabbalistic instances of *zimzum* confirm the intuitions of Scholem and the tentative intimations explored by Idel. The Alexandrian Valentinus, who Christianized Gnosticism, seems to me as Judahistic as Jesus, whether in his eloquent *The Gospel of Truth,* or in the fragmentary poems that are the literary Sublime of Gnostic tradition until this day.

THE GREAT NAHMANIDES (1194–1270) was the principal spiritual authority of Spanish Jewry in his day, and his own turn to Kabbalah made it possible for this apparent esotericism to gain an audience first in Catalonia and then in Castile. *Zimzum* was grafted from midrash onto Kabbalah by Nahmanides, and the concept widened so that by a century or so later Shem Tov ben Shem Tov quotes an anonymous precursor's marvelous transformation of creation:

> The Name, our Lord, blessed be He, who is One, Unique and Special, because all needs Him, and He does not need them, His knowledge is united to Him and there is nothing outside Him. And He is called 'Aleph, the head of all the letters, corresponding to the fact that He is One . . . and how did He innovate and create the world? Like a man who comprises his spirit and concentrates his spirit, and the world remains in darkness, and within this darkness He chopped rocks and chiseled cliffs in order to extract from there the paths called "Wonders of Wisdom," and this is the meaning of the verse "He took out light from the hiddenness," and this is the secret of "a dark fire on the white fire," and this is the secret of "face and back."

Moshe Idel, in his *Absorbing Perfections: Kabbalah and Interpretation* (2002), says that such vital "darkness" results from a kind of divine excavation (page 53). I find the passage disturbing because God has held in his breath in order to create a dark matter from which he can sculpt rocky cliffs into paths of wisdom we will never walk upon.

In Moses Cordovero the concept of *zimzum* is present but not central. Swerving from his teacher, Isaac Luria captured this metaphor forever. And yet Luria seems to have written only one minor work, a Cordoveran commentary on a section of the *Zohar*. The Lurianic Speculation (as we might call it) was an oral tradition, communicated to various disciples, and they do not agree upon its details. A messianic figure, Luria remains a legend in Jewish tradition. Four major disciples propounded his teachings: Hayyim Vital, Joseph Ibn Tabul, Moses Jonah, and Israel Sarug. Some of the problems in finding the "authentic" vision of Jesus repeat themselves in regard to Luria, another messianic "son of Joseph."

Yahweh is my concern and not Luria, but I seek to apprehend the abyss within the Tanakh's Yahweh by way of the Lurianic radical revision of Yahweh-as-creator. As with Walt Whitman in *Leaves of Grass* (in which Scholem located fascinating analogues to Kabbalah), it is virtually impossible for me to separate out the literal from the metaphorical in Isaac Luria. To that exalted consciousness, who held conversations with the Sages in their graves in Safed, such a distinction could not exist, while Whitman desires his readers to tease out literal from figurative for themselves.

So subtle was Luria in his oral teachings that we may not be able any longer to apprehend his vision of creation, disaster, and the redemption of mending, though Lawrence Fine, generously acknowledging the giants of Kabbalah scholarship, Scholem and Idel, seems to me in this an advance on everything prior to him.

The cosmological myth Isaac Luria taught is without doubt the most elaborate such story in all of Jewish tradition. It certainly bears no resemblance to the brevity and elegant simplicity of the biblical account of creation, and even in comparison to the far more complex cosmogonic myth of Spanish Kabbalah, Luria's teachings are extraordinarily intricate. While we tend to think of a creation myth in terms of a single, coherent narrative that can be told as one does a simple story, Luria's mythological teachings have not come down to us in this way. Instead, we discover a seemingly endless series of inordinately complex notions, presented in often fragmentary and conflicting versions by multiple authors and editors. (p. 124)

As Fine observes, the problem is as much Luria's dialectical intensities as the contradictory (even self-contradictory) rival versions given by his disciples. What fascinates me, and constitutes a crucial insight into Yahweh, is that Luria saw *zimzum* as a *perpetual* process going on in God, taking place with each inhalation and exhalation of the divine breath. Try to imagine that every time you hold your breath, and then release it, you create and ruin another world.

Dead at thirty-eight, Luria can be considered as a poetic genius whose achievement was truncated, but what we possess of his teachings, however distorted they may be in his disciples' versions, continues to irradiate all subsequent Jewish religious speculation. Here I want to take his myth of creation and apply it directly to the uncanniness of Yahweh, a knowingly preposterous quest on my part, in more than one sense of "preposterous." The prophets of Judaism in my own lifetime whom I most wholeheartedly accept are Gershom Scholem (1897–1982) and Moshe Idel (born in 1947). Scholem, in his "Ten Unhistorical Aphorisms on Kabbalah" (first printed, in German, in 1958), insisted that *all* authentic spiritual tradition remains hidden, and that speech and writing protect secrets better than silence does. Since Yahweh himself is the Torah, it must be as unknowable as God is. According to Scholem, Luria's doctrines are literally true, as well as metaphorically, so Yahweh is as much subject to divine degradation as he is in the Valentinian Gnostic speculation or in Nathan of Gaza's heretical *Treatise on the Dragons*. There has to be an abyss in the will of Yahweh, since without a negative moment in the act of creation, God and the cosmos would fuse as one. The Law (Torah), seen by a Kabbalistic light, is already antinomian, yet even Kabbalah is marred by its Neoplatonic theory of emanation, in which the divine fullness brims and overflows. This was corrected by the Gnosis of Moses Cordovero and of Luria, in which Yahweh and his divine will brush each other but do not coincide. Even Yahweh must be seen at that place where each of us takes her or his stance, so the magical *tikkun,* or "mending," of Luria is no more or less valid than the utopian, Marxist messianism of Scholem's lifelong best friend, the critic Walter Benjamin. And since the name Yahweh "can be pronounced but not expressed," it requires mediation by tradition if even we are to hear it, and only quasi-occult fragments of the true name can reach us, just as uninterpretable as the fragments of Franz Kafka, who, Scholem tells us, was the secular heir of Kabbalah, and whose writings have for us "something of the strong light of the canonical, of that perfection which destroys."

As Yahweh, Torah cannot be read, and even its inaugural author, J, or the Yahwist, is not less esoteric than Luria. And that is my starting point for defying biblical scholarship in order to search for the *zimzum* already implicit in the Yahwist's saga. Literary criticism, as I practice it, consists in making the implicit into what we also need to experience explicitly. But I turn back first to summarizing Luria on creation, following the guidance of Scholem and of Lawrence Fine in particular.

ANY CONCENTRATION of Yahweh's overwhelming presence pragmatically must also be a contraction, or there could be no reality except God's, and no evil either. Perhaps Yahweh wearied of his own rigor and sought a vacation from reality? That is a touch outrageous, but recall always that Yahweh is a human god and not a theological entity. Yahweh had not read Plato.

Abandoned in the void left by the *zimzum* was a mass of Yahweh's judgmental strictness that ironically produced the first Golem, a prehuman monster of mindless matter. Like Walt Whitman's, Yahweh's agonies were only changes of garments. Perhaps in aesthetic revulsion (purely my surmise) Yahweh darted a beam of light into the wretched Golem, and thus created Adam Kadmon, the androgyne and primal human. Transpose that back to the J Writer's account of creation and a new perspective opens for us confronting Genesis 2:7:

> Yahweh formed Adam from the *adamah* [dust of the earth's moistened red clay] and blew into Adam's nostrils the breath of life, and man became a living being.

In Luria's vision, we began as the Golem, and then Yahweh's hand and breath shaped us. After a profound inhalation *(zimzum)*, Yahweh had additional breath with which to vivify us. Scholem, pondering Lurianic myth, saw metaphors for Sephardic exile from Iberia, but Idel gently reminded us that Luria was Ashkenazi, and Fine emphasizes that sixteenth-century Safed already was a community of mystical fellowship before Luria's advent as a messianic inspiration. Luria's genius gave him a new and unique insight into the mind of God. This makes me wonder if the Lurianic story of creation can give us perpetually fresh perceptions of Yahweh's personality and character, just as the Gospel of Mark seems to me the text where the enigmas of Jesus are best explored.

Luria's Ein-Sof begins in an absolute solitude of light. The writings of Ronit Meroz, mostly not yet available in English, are the fullest I have seen on Luria's creativity, and I strongly recommend Meroz's essay "Faithful Transmission Versus Innovation" in Luria and his disciples, printed in the *Proceedings* of an international congress on the fiftieth anniversary of Scholem's classic *Major Trends in Jewish Mysticism* (Tübingen, 1993). Lawrence Fine, acknowledging Meroz, presents a lucid account of Lurianic myth on pages 124–49 of *Physician of the Soul, Healer of the Cosmos,* to which I am indebted in some of what follows here.

Why does Yahweh choose to abandon his solitary, irradiated existence? Though Luria does not explicitly say so, his myth stimulates me to wonder if that lonely light had become dangerously oppressive for a God without end, limitless in his self-sufficiency. Yahweh is uniquely *the* human god, but I will expound upon that in my next chapter on his psychology.

WHAT IS MOST DISTURBING about Yahweh is his highly ambivalent attitude toward his own creation. For a God all-powerful— unlike Zeus and Odin—Yahweh is perpetually and surprisingly anxious. All Bible readers learn quite rapidly that God's actions are not predictable. The extraordinary explanatory usefulness of Kabbalah, particularly of Luria's, for me rises from the virtual identity of Yahweh and *zimzum*. As a metaphor, *zimzum* might seem a peculiar candidate for fusion with the divine, but just as Yahweh is as literal as life and death, yet also he is figurative, even in his name, so *zimzum* is both a literal inhalation of breath and of being, and an image of what defies linguistic description, God's initial catastrophe-creation of a primal abyss.

Reprising the sinuous argument of Gershom Scholem's subversive "Ten Unhistorical Aphorisms on Kabbalah" should clarify the project of seeking a new comprehension of Yahweh's ambiguities. Like all authentic traditions concerning him, Yahweh remains the hidden God, hedged about by the Tanakh, the two Talmuds, and Kabbalah. And since Yahweh himself is Torah, the Talmuds, the *Zohar,* and the entire Oral Law from Moses to Isaac Luria, all of them are finally as unknowable as he is. That serves to fence off Jewish Gnosis from Basilides, Valentinus, and all Gnosticism after them, including Shi'ite Sufism, Christian Catharism, and much of the Romantic poetry of the Western Canon.

Since Luria's story of *zimzum* and its consequent Breaking of the Vessels is literal truth, then Yahweh permanently wounded himself very badly by and in the act of creation. A self-degraded Supreme God, so human-all-too-human, forever will be ambivalent toward everything and anyone, his Chosen People in particular. If indeed they were his intended nation even *before* his travail, he will alternately balance and favor them, depending upon his whims. On his bad days, their praises and Temple offerings scarcely will suffice.

We all live with an abyss in our own wills: Hamlet exemplifies our condition, and few of us can match his prowess in thinking his way through to the nihilistic truth that annihilates. Yet we share Hamlet's dilemmas; we too need to be nothing and everything, in ourselves, when we must face Yahweh (death) in a final confrontation. St. Paul insisted that the last enemy to be overcome would be death, but Paul lived and was martyred before Luria permanently fused Yahweh and *zimzum.* The Gnostics that Paul opposed, particularly at Corinth, were nowhere that formidable.

Luria turned the opacity of Mosaic Law into a transparency in which Yahweh's limitations are exposed. Scholem, disdaining the Neoplatonism of early Kabbalah with its orderly emanation of *Sefirot,* urged the truth of Cordovero's and Luria's Jewish Gnosticism, which divides Yahweh off from the Mosaic Judaic myth of the Will of God. To Moses, Yahweh willed whatever he would. In our America, Jesus, and the Holy Ghost in Pentecostalism, touch that Will but decidedly do not coincide with it. The American Jesus and the rapidly burgeoning Paraclete are free to raise Cain both at home and abroad, all in the unwarranted name of Yahweh, who is not to be mocked with impunity, as we are bound to learn again. Isaac Luria, to the surprise of his disciples, explicitly redeemed Cain, who had been ransomed long before his birth, by the *zimzum.*

The scary greatness of Scholem is that he masked as a historian of esoteric religion, while slyly growing into a prophet of Jewish Gnosticism, a Cordovero or Luria for the twentieth century, whose catastrophes are not abating during our early years of the twenty-first. It is not clear whether the God of Gershom Scholem's Kabbalah is utopian and hopeful or magical and mischievous, or perhaps all of those. Canonical religious writings—Christian, Jewish, Muslim, Hindu, Buddhist, even Taoist—radiate a perfection and strict light that destroys us, however devotedly we labor to absorb it. Even if the American Jesus truly is Yahweh's son, who among us is holy enough to sustain that light?

18.

YAHWEH'S PSYCHOLOGY

IF YAHWEH, on a gigantic scale, has a human shape, and is or once was Man, then some insight into him may be reachable through the Kabbalah's tripartite division of the soul: *nephesh, ruach, neshamah.* Adopting Walt Whitman's Kabbalah (as Gershom Scholem named it to me), what are Yahweh's "Myself," "Real Me or Me Myself," and "Soul"? Let us imagine a Whitmanian Yahweh proclaiming:

I believe in you my soul
The other I Am must not abase itself to you
And you must not be abased to the other

Like Yahweh, like Walt: the "I" is the great "I Am That I Am," *ehyeh asher ehyeh, "ehyeh"* ("I Will Be") punning upon the ultimate name, Yahweh, the Tetragrammaton YHWH. More outrageously (even), Yahweh could say, "Yahweh, one of the roughs, an Israelite." How piquant it might be to have Yahweh describe "the other I Am," "Real

Me or Me Myself" as "Both in and out of the game and watching and wondering at it," whether at Mamre or the Cities of the Plain or Peniel or on Sinai.

YAHWEH'S *NEPHESH,* or soul, might be called the Supreme Fiction, God's persona outered to mediate between his own living being and his unknowable *neshamah,* the soul that is a mystery even to him. Somehow between Yahweh's *nephesh* and *neshamah* there intervenes his Shekhinah, dwelling within him in precarious union with his own *ruach,* vital inner breath. In God as in Man (according to the *Zohar*) the initial part of the soul is the *nephesh,* origin of all consciousness. But only Yahweh and elite spirits among us manifest *ruach,* as a full sense of holiness is attained, partly from Torah study, at which God himself is adept. *Neshamah,* Yahweh's own soul, is the highest mode, reserved for masters of Kabbalah.

Originally the categories of Jewish Neoplatonism, informed by Aristotle on the mind, these three grades of consciousness became so variously defined that no consistency adheres to them. Something like the "spark," or *pneuma,* of the Gnostics survives in the *neshamah,* Yahweh-within-us. In Lurianic Kabbalah, a bewildering multiplication of the sparks defies any rapid summary. But as before, Yahweh himself is my concern. What can be learned of this disconcertingly human God from his own psychic cartography and its vicissitudes?

Pre-Kabbalistic tradition, perhaps more startling than Kabbalah itself, insists that Torah, in its true, proper order (unknown to us), constitutes the accurate name of Yahweh, of which the Tetragrammaton

YHWH gives only a hint. In the Oral Torah received by Moses at Sinai, the actual name was fully revealed, with the warning that it had the power of miracle, even of resurrecting the dead. Torah is the Great Name of Yahweh himself, unifying his tripartite consciousness of being, and indeed constituting his body. But as Scholem delighted in observing, Torah, like Yahweh, cannot be known. Jesus—who at once replaced Temple, Torah, and Yahweh—is known to so many Americans (in particular) that all too early we can lose the numinous sense of God's unknowability.

The Kabbalah of Gershom Scholem strongly emphasizes hearing God over seeing him, perhaps more a Jewish than Greek mode of apprehension. In *Through a Speculum That Shines* (1994), Elliot R. Wolfson argues instead for visionary gnosis as being more central to Kabbalah. A disciple of William Blake in my far-off youth, I am receptive to Wolfson's orientation, though a little skeptical as to *seeing* the Names Divine even when written in black fire upon white fire. Yet Wolfson's insights are stimulating on a central problem concerning Yahweh: he keeps his visibility while insisting he cannot and must not be seen:

> [T]he Jewish mystics are primarily interpreters of scripture. The preoccupation with visualizing the divine stems directly from the anxiety of influence of biblical theophanies. (p. 394)

For Wolfson, "the seeing of God in Jewish mysticism is intensely eroticized." Moshe Idel's forthcoming *Kabbalah and Eros* confirms Wolfson's passionate rejection of a largely auditory Yahweh. Following both Wolfson and Idel, I leap here to a direct confrontation between the Yahwistic-Whitmanian and Shakespearean-Freudian maps of the mind. An erotically driven Yahweh who nevertheless possesses no lust (since the Shekhinah at least begins as an inward dwelling presence) seems to me pragmatically Whitmanian, like the autoerotic poet of *Song of Myself* and "Spontaneous Me." Freudian Man is radically incomplete: like Shakespeare's women and men, he must fall in love or choke on his overfilled inner self, the fate of poor Malvolio in *Twelfth Night,* of the widower Shylock, and even more of the unloving Hamlet. Yahweh, like Walt Whitman, does not need to fall in love with any individual, though King David comes closest to almost moving the solitary Hebrew God. Whitman, whatever happened to him in some kind of homoerotic debacle in the winter of 1859–60, truly emulates Yahweh's relation to the Shekhinah by internalizing his Fancy—the Interior Paramour, as Wallace Stevens named the Muse he involuntarily shared with Whitman. Shakespeare's and Freud's major protagonists are not primarily poets, but Yahweh is. Rabbi Akiba ben Joseph, rabbi-of-rabbis forever, insisted that Solomon's Song of Songs be canonized, because he interpreted it as Yahweh's own poem of ecstatic courtship, the "my sister, my spouse" being the Shekhinah. Yahweh is more Freudian in sharing the death-drive of *Beyond the Pleasure Principle,* where I've mentioned previously that Freud invented and then rejected the concept of *destrudo,* a negative libido we might all go about thinking we possessed had Freud stayed with the notion. *Contra* Freud, libido is a myth: there is no separate sexual energy. Yahweh, like Balzac's men and women, subsumes his supposed libido by a general energetics. Freud, though he stubbornly insisted he knew nothing of Schopenhauer, exalts a will-to-live far more de-structive than Yahweh needs to indulge.

Macbeth was Freud's favorite identity in Shakespeare, possibly be-cause the drive beyond the pleasure principle scarcely could venture further—Yahweh's surrogate in Shakespeare is King Lear, who infuri-ated Tolstoy and who marks a limit of literary art. Outward self, Real Me, and soul break apart in the magnificent king, as they do in the Yahweh of Exodus and Numbers, who angrily guides his covenanted people in a mad march through the Wilderness, en route from Egypt to Canaan. There isn't any apt term for Yahweh's relation to his own *neshamah,* or soul. Since he is, also, more a literary character than were Whitman and Freud, I am now uneasy in talking about "the psychol-ogy of Yahweh." He won't go away, though I wish he would, since to think of him is to remember my own mortality. And yet in Kabbalah we are told that God is primordial Man. The *Zohar* says that our obli-gation is to pierce the garment both of Torah and of God, but how? At birth, the *nephesh* enters us, but Yahweh (unlike Jesus) is not born. Still, if *zimzum,* or self-contraction, was his origin, just as it was ours, we can speculate that God's first sharp intake of breath inaugurated his *nephesh.* His *ruach* presumably began when he vivified Adam, but what gave him a first awareness of his own *nephesh?* Evidently, his union with the Shekhinah, or his own female component, pragmatically creates his overt consciousness of his own, higher soul.

There are few (if any) parallels to that in Shakespeare and in Freud, though there certainly is a Whitmanian analogue early in *Song of Myself.* D. H. Lawrence, who like Whitman created a Kabbalah en-tirely his own, gave us a Jesus who similarly finds his higher soul in the late, short novel *The Man Who Died.* An English Nonconformist by religious upbringing, Lawrence vastly offended T. S. Eliot in Eliot's primer of modern heresy, *After Strange Gods.*

What can be ventured as to the knowledge attained by Yahweh of his own soul? If *zimzum* inaugurated both cosmos and God himself as Yahweh truncated down to Elohim, then he began with an ambivalence toward creation, men and women included. The history of the Jews is a hecatomb to that ambivalence toward the Chosen. Anyone who ponders the Hebrew Bible can wonder why Yahweh never laments that he has forsaken himself.

The prophetic litany throughout the Tanakh is that the Jewish people have betrayed their Covenant with Yahweh. Not once are we told the other and more awful truth: God's destruction of his covenanted people. As I have mentioned, Gershom Scholem, in a rare mistake, associated Isaac Luria's visions of *zimzum* and *shevirat ha-kelim* with the Iberian expulsion of the Jews, which had no direct relevance to the Ashkenazi Ari, as the lion-like Luria was known. But as almost always, Scholem imaginatively recaptured the Gnostic elements in Kabbalah, which implicitly addresses itself to God's soul and his absences from it.

(2)

In the long history of the Jews, there is no more disturbing figure than the false Messiah Jacob Frank (1726–1791), whose sect, most but not all of them Catholic converts, existed in Poland and elsewhere until at least the late nineteenth century and may survive in a few remnants today. Jacob Frank represented the last stand of the false Messiah Shabbetai Zevi (1626–1676) of Smyrna, who converted to Islam in 1666, bringing along many of his followers. Shabbetai's prophet, Nathan of Gaza (1643–1680), defended Shabbetai's apostasy as a mystical necessity (which Nathan himself, however, did not adopt) and composed a wholly Gnostic Kabbalah that remains the most radical doctrine of God's own apostasy in Jewish tradition. In Nathan of Gaza's *Treatise on the Dragons,* the Messiah's psyche suffers ultimate degradation, a way down and out that will lead ultimately to the way up:

> Know that the soul of the messianic king exists in the lower *golem.* For just as the primal dragon emerged in the vacant space, even so the soul of the messiah was created by the will of God. This soul existed before the creation of the world, and it remains in the great abyss.

Jacob Frank, whose spirit also coiled below with the dragons, was regarded as the low point of Jewish history by the most idiosyncratic of the Hasidic masters, Rabbi Nahman of Bratslav, who remains still the final guide of the surviving Bratslavians. That was a unique distinction until the fairly recent refusal of the numerous Lubavitchers to choose a replacement for their late *rebbe,* Menachem Schneerson. The two masters each possess messianic eminence for their followers.

I invoke the extraordinary Nahman of Bratslav here because he possessed more considerable insights into what I would call the tormented psychology of God than anyone since Isaac Luria. Nahman was a great-grandson of the Baal Shem Tov ("master of the good name"), the founder of Hasidism, but his personality diverged sharply from the ecstatic joyousness of his ancestors. Emotionally turbulent, a depressive self-tormentor, Nahman was a literary genius, whose carefully formed allegorical tales and *obiter dicta* retain their rhetorical power.

Nahman says little about his great-grandfather, and no dialogue would have been possible between them. Reading the Bratslaver *rebbe*, I feel frequently I am inside one of Robert Browning's dramatic monologues, say, *Childe Roland to the Dark Tower Came*. For Nahman also, the quest moves through all things deformed and broken, until unaware you come upon the place. After a lifetime training for the sight, you confront a void, from which the object of your quest has departed. Ringed by the living frame of your forerunners (Zohar, Luria, and the Baal Shem Tov among them), you confront the absence of God. However heroic your response (read the extraordinary thirteen tales Nahman composed), you transcend either victory or defeat. How much of Yahweh survives in Nahman, who regarded himself as the Messiah?

God in the Bratslaver is not merely an absence dwindled down from a presence. After one *zimzum* too many, Yahweh shrunk into Elohim cannot be distinguished from the cosmic void he wanders. Torah, which is Yahweh, has been revised into Nahman's interpretations, which are totally free except as regards the Mosaic domain of right conduct. There is no antinomianism in Nahman, nothing of Shabbetai Zevi's or Jacob Frank's libertine excess. The moral Law prevails, but its giver, who was Being itself, has vaporized into the void of Jewish dispersion and suffering.

A Talmudic maxim says of Yahweh, "He is the place *(makom)* of the world, but the world is not his place." Nahman relied on a darker wisdom: the world is a place from which God has withdrawn. The Breaking of the Vessels is for Nahman the more crucial Lurianic vision.

An endlessly contracting Yahweh ensues in a breathless God, whose final silence may well be that of someone whose pharynx is bad. His voice gone, Yahweh may still be visible, but only as Daniel's Ancient of Days, hardly the robust trickster of the J Writer's saga. But visible or invisible, God is not for Nahman an auditory guide, if a guide is required at all by this most inward of Messiahs, at least since Yeshua of Nazareth.

In her poignant novel *The Seventh Beggar* (2004), Pearl Abraham completes Nahman's most famous tale, "The Seven Beggars," which the Master deliberately left unfinished. In "The Seven Beggars," the enigmatic *shnorrers* (who are both ancient and youthful) tell stories they somehow recall, even though each also could say, *Ikh gedenk gornisht* ("I can't remember a thing!"). Platonic intimations of God's prebirth existence are evoked, with the Bratslaver twist shrewdly expounded by Arthur Green: the whole cosmos, and all of us, were as originary as Yahweh. Creation itself goes back before *the* Creation. Yet only six of the seven Platonic beggars tells his tale; the lame one (generally identified with Nahman himself) does not arrive, for that would mean the Messiah's self-revelation, the troubled Nahman's vindication. Pearl Abraham courageously tells the story:

And when the six tales were told, the travelers turned toward me, the beggar without feet, and wondered how without feet I could have traveled far enough to find a tale worth telling. And I told them a tale of seven pilgrims who walked the deserts and steppes, over mountains, hills, and dales, through fields and streams, in the icy cold of winters and the scalding heat of summers, and while they walked they talked. And exhausted themselves with walking and talking and listening and telling. And I told their six tales word for word, as they had been told to me. And when I arrived at the seventh tale, the tale of the beggar without feet, I told a tale of seven travelers walking, trudging and grudging, tired and mired in leaves and mud, and so forth. And all the while talking, telling tales. And I told the tales these pilgrims told, word for word I told their tales, and then I told my tale: a tale of seven wanderers. And it was agreed that I the beggar without feet, slow and trailing behind, was nevertheless farther and deeper traveled, because within my tale were contained all tales. And I talked and walked, and with every step, between one step and the next, I dreamed a dream. And in one dream I awoke and saw that the Leviathan had not yet emerged, the story could not be finished. I walked onward, another step, another tale, another dream. Between dream and dream I awoke and found myself in this wedding pit and in this pit among the wedding guests, was the prince who had stumbled into heresy, but as long as he was here, as long as he listened and believed the tales, his wisdom and heresy were restrained. He listened and rejoiced much as his father, the old King, had once rejoiced. To prevent another stumble, I, the beggar without feet, must continue. I pause only to present your wedding gift, that you may be as I am.

If Job's Leviathan, or death, God's sanctified tyranny of nature over man, has not yet emerged, then Kabbalah's promise that at the Redemption we all of us, Job and the *Zohar*'s mystical companions, will feast upon the formerly dread creature cannot yet be fulfilled. The bride and bridegroom nevertheless are a new Eve and Adam, the stumbling prince is Nahman of Bratslav, and the old King is Yahweh in his guise as Ancient of Days. If stumbling, heresy, and wisdom all are one, that is because Yahweh himself stumbled into the heresy of the Breaking of the Vessels. Even as the Lurianic Ein-Sof fuses with his perpetual acts of *zimzum*, so are *all* of his acts further breakings of the vessels.

Nahman's greatest originality, his great swerve from Lurianic Kabbalah, was to deny the *reshimu*, the remnant of God's light that stayed behind in the void of the *tehiru*, the space vacated by Yahweh in the initial *zimzum*. Without the saving remnant of divine light, we stumble about in the void, beggars with amputated feet. How much of Yahweh's soul survives the perpetual Breaking of the Vessels? Holding in his breath, the old King is in perpetual suspension, deserting his Chosen as the worlds go on ruining. Whatever this Yahweh has become, it is a final irony to call him limitless, to name him: "Without End."

IF GOD HIMSELF as Elohim is a catastrophe creation, then he rightly transcends the esoteric Jewish myth that says he made and ruined many a world before this one. Still, the Sages did us little good by scrubbing Yahweh of his imperfections. There are advantages, moral and aesthetic, of identifying Yahweh as pre-*zimzum* and as the void or abyss that results from the Breaking of the Vessels. A breathless, hard-breathing Yahweh, perpetually contracting and withdrawing into Elohim, retains his dynamism and his ill-temper. We (many among us) would like him to go away but he won't. Freud said we had to make friends with the necessity of dying, a Yahwistic observation, though I prefer Montaigne's advice: Don't bother to prepare for your death because, when the time comes, you will know how to do it well enough.

A Christian *believes* that Jesus was the Christ, anointed before the creation in order to atone for the sins of this world. Muslims *submit* to Allah's will, shatteringly set forth in the Qur'an. My own mother *trusted in* the Covenant, despite Yahweh's blatant violation of its terms. Shakespeare could never have put Yahweh on stage, but did the next best substitute portrayal, of King Lear, who could well be analyzed by the myths of Lurianic Kabbalah. Call Lear's abdication his *zimzum,* and his madness and furies a Breaking of the Vessels.

(3)

Freud endorsed erotic substitution as our second chance that might begin to heal the narcissistic scar of having lost the initial object of desire, the parent of the opposite gender to the parent of the same gender. I tend to interpret *zimzum* as "substitution" in something like the Freudian sense. By contracting, Yahweh substitutes his own Will for at least part of his own Being. That substitution is surely no easy matter for God: indeed even before Luria, there were traditions that Yahweh's name was always pre-*zimzum,* and that after contraction, he becomes Elohim. Note that as the Fullness of Being, God remains

Yahweh. His Will, withdrawn from him, is called Elohim. Scholem insisted that without the negative moment of *zimzum,* God and the cosmos fuse as one. Idel traces in archaic Jewish fragmentary texts the origins of *zimzum,* an idea that Cordovero inherited and then passed on to Luria. Though some students of Scholem still resent Idel, and an informed literary scholar like Robert Alter attempted to dismiss Idel, time's perspectives begin to show us that Idel is closer to Scholem's own spirit than the disciples are. Scholem desired a Gnostic Kabbalah, free of the emanationist theosophies of Neoplatonism, and Idel persuasively shows us that Gnosticism is largely a parody of fascinating elements in archaic Judaisms. He bases this upon archaic texts, including the different versions of the Books of Enoch, in which the division between God and man at times seems abolished.

What the stances of both Scholem and Idel teach is that Yahweh's psychology becomes further humanized by his drive to create a cosmos and men and women separate from himself. Implicit in them also, and made powerfully explicit by scholars like Yehuda Liebes and Elliot Wolfson, is the peculiar power of Christian Kabbalah, which found in Jesus Christ a second *zimzum,* which could be called a further contraction of Elohim or Adonai down to the level of the Trinity's God the Father. If Jack Miles wishes to see Christ as a crisis in the life of God, I would agree with him, but only on the premise that the God involved is not the originary Yahweh but rather God the Father, a shadow of Yahweh. One step further on, and you come to our American moment, where God the Father has faded away, yielding both to the American Jesus and to his increasingly strong rival, the Holy Spirit of our Pentecostalism, which richly mixes Hispanics, African-Americans, and dispossessed urban and Southern whites.

A newer sociology of American religion might found itself on an intellectual reflection upon the metaphor of Yahweh's two-staged *zimzum*, first to Elohim, and then to God the Father sacrificing his son for the common good. The American Jesus may become too compromised by the Christian Right to go on as the intimate friend of the dispossessed. The Holy Spirit may yet be the reigning divinity of the United States of America (oddly prophesied long ago in Thomas Pynchon's *The Crying Lot of 49*).

19

IRRECONCILABILITY OF CHRISTIANITY AND JUDAISM

T HAT EVEN THE TITLE of this section will seem unfortu-
nate to many readers is an oddity, after two thousand years of
plain fact. There are doubtless political and social benefits, ongoing
and crucial, that stem from the myth of "the Judeo-Christian tradition," but delusions finally prove pernicious, as they did for German-
speaking Jewry. "Christian-Jewish dialogue" isn't even a myth, but
invariably farce. Jacob Neusner, our supreme scholar of Jewish writings from the first century before the Common Era on through at
least the sixth century that were unhappily shared by Jews and Christians, pungently says that the two religions represent "different
people talking about different things to different people" (*Jews and
Christians: The Myth of a Common Tradition,* 1991, 1–15).

This difference, that certainly has made a difference, begins with
the sharp contrast classically outlined by Martin Buber. Jews are not
asked to *believe* but rather to *trust* in the Covenant cut between Yahweh
and the Patriarchs and Prophets, from Noah and Abraham through

Moses on to Jeremiah and finally the rabbi-of-rabbis, Akiba ben Joseph. Christians *believe* that Joshua ben Joseph was the Messiah, the God Jesus Christ, who was incarnated miraculously in the womb of Miriam, his virgin mother, and who now reigns in eternity as the viceroy of God his Father, in the company also of the Holy Spirit, hosts of angels, and the multitudes he has redeemed and saved.

This Christian God the Father has only the slightest resemblance to Yahweh, God Himself, named Allah in the Qur'an, and called on under several other names in Asia and in Africa. Nietzsche warned us to ask always, "Who is the interpreter and what power does he seek to gain over the text?"

There is a superb paragraph in Jacob Neusner that seems to me the beginning of wisdom in contrasting those rival Gods (in my judgment) Jesus and Yahweh:

> When, for example, Jesus asked people who they thought he was, the enigmatic answer proved less interesting than the question posed. For the task he set himself, as portrayed by not only the Gospels but also Paul and the other New Testament writers, was to reframe everything people know through encounter with what they did not know: a taxonomic enterprise. When the rabbis of late antiquity rewrote in their own image and likeness the entire scripture and history of Israel, dropping whole eras as though they had never been, ignoring vast bodies of old Jewish writing, inventing whole new books for the canon of Judaism, they did the same thing. They reworked what they had received in light of what they proposed to give. (*Jews and Christians,* p. 102)

That is the Jesus of the Gospel of Mark, who interests me most, together with the Jesus of the quasi-Gnostic Gospel of Thomas. What absorbs me far less than the original Yahweh of the J Writer, author of what are the earliest layers of the palimpsest of Genesis, Exodus, and Numbers, is the Judaism Neusner rightly sees as the invention of Akiba and his fellow rabbis of the second century of the Common Era. Their post-Christian religion (weird as that must sound) bases itself upon a persuasively strong misreading of Tanakh meant to confront the desperate needs of a Jewish people occupied and terrorized by the Roman Empire. The Temple had been destroyed by the Romans in 70 C.E., and most of Jerusalem with it. In 135 C.E., after the Roman Holocaust that followed the massive Bar Kochba rebellion, Israel's last stand before 1947, Jerusalem was obliterated and Akiba was martyred, at the age of ninety-five, by the abominable Hadrian, who massacred more Jews than anyone else in history before Hitler. Christianity had replaced the Temple by the person of Jesus Christ, while Akiba rebuilt the Temple in every Jewish household. Yahweh, who still feels homeless after his Temple's destruction, seems to me to have exiled himself, somewhere in the outer spaces, until he returned to Israel in 1948. In the year 2004, when I write, one can only hope that he does not demand his Temple again, since Al Aksa Mosque stands upon its site, and we have quite enough religious war already without what could prove to be that final catastrophe. Zealots in Jerusalem and scattered throughout American Protestant Fundamentalism conspire incessantly to destroy the inconvenient mosque, and suitably pure red heifers are being bred in the United States as potential sacrifices to lure Yahweh back to his Temple grounds.

I mention this well-attested madness only to confess my uneasy waning of skepticism in regard to Yahweh. Doubting his continued existence is a rational exercise, but he hardly is a static entity, like the Christian Father-God. His fearsome dynamism renders even his absences into potential disturbances.

If Jesus Christ, true God and true man, is impossibly remote from Yahweh (as presumably Yeshua of Nazareth was not), this is because Greek theological formulations and Hebraic experiential memories simply are antithetical to each other.

20.

CONCLUSION:
REALITY-TESTING

D EPLORING RELIGION is as useless as celebrating it. Where shall transcendence be found? There are the arts: Shakespeare, Bach, Michelangelo still suffice for an elite, but hardly for entire peoples. Yahweh, under whatever name, Allah included, is not quite the universal divinity of a globe bound together by instantaneous information, yet he lingers on, all but everywhere. Jesus is closer to universality, but his thousand guises are too bewildering for coherence. Freud, the final Victorian or Edwardian prophet, underestimated Yahweh, Jesus, and Muhammad. He thought them illusive, and saw little future for them. It seems ironic that the greatest of Jewish geniuses (since Jesus anyway) failed to apprehend the permanent power of texts that cannot vanish: Tanakh, New Testament, Qur'an. If asked the desert island question, I would have to take Shakespeare, but the world continues drowning in the blood-dimmed tide of its scriptures, whether it reads them or not.

Yahweh, whom I have evaded throughout my three-quarters of a century, has an awesome capacity not to go away, though he deserves to be convicted for desertion, in regard not just to the Jews but to all suffering humankind. In this book the interpreter is a Jew whose spirituality responds most fervently to the ancient tendency we term Gnosticism, which may or may not be a "religion" in the sense that Judaism, Christianity, and Islam remain the primary Western traditions. I very much want to dismiss Yahweh as the ancient Gnostics did, finding in him a mere demiurge who had botched the Creation so that it was simultaneously a Fall. But I wake up these days, sometime between midnight and two A.M., because of nightmares in which Yahweh sardonically appears as various beings, ranging from a Havana-smoking, Edwardian-attired Dr. Sigmund Freud to the Book of Daniel's silently reproachful Ancient of Days. I trudge downstairs gloomily and silently, lest I wake my wife, and breakfast on tea and dark bread while rereading yet once more in the Tanakh, wide swatches of Mishnah and Talmud, and those disquieting texts the New Testament and Augustine's *City of God.* At times, in writing this book, I defend myself only by murmuring Oscar Wilde's apothegm that life is too important to be taken seriously. Yahweh, I ruefully would add, is much too important to be taken ironically, even if irony can seem as much *his* own mode as it is Prince Hamlet's.

I both admire and am rendered ironic by a recent cogent yet self-curtailing book, *The End of Faith: Religion, Terror, and the Future of Reason,* by Sam Harris (2004), a neuroscientist and secular humanist, who is rightly anxious for the future of American democracy. Pragmatically, I do not differ from Harris, but I part from him when he asks evidence for "the literal existence of Yahweh." Creator and destroyer, Yahweh stands remote from the inner cosmos of neuroscience. He contains, and cannot be contained. Reason is not an instrument for dislodging him, however admirably that might extend democracy and limit Muslim terror and American and Israeli counterterror, or what could yet be the horror of Hindu-Muslim nuclear exchanges, or of Israeli preemptive obliteration in Tehran. Yahweh, though evident only as a literary character, reduced us to the status of minor literary characters, supporting casts for the protagonist-of-protagonists in a universe of death. He mocks our mortality in the Book of Job: we are dramatically unpersuasive when we mock him, and self-destructive when, like Ahab, we harpoon Leviathan, king over all the children of pride.

Yahweh sanctifies the tyranny of nature over women and men: that is the harsh wisdom of Job's tale. St. Paul, a Hebrew of the Hebrews, tells us the last enemy to be overcome is death. Skeptics, confronting Islam, are quite likely to agree with Sam Harris: "Islam . . . has all the makings of a thoroughgoing cult of death" (page 123). Harris cites polls of opinion in Muslim countries totally refuting our platitudes that suicide bombers are not supported by substantial majorities of Muslims: most certainly they are. If Yahweh is a man of war, Allah is a suicide bomber.

(2)

Yet how different are Freud's "reality-testing" and Sam Harris's "Nothing is more sacred than the facts"? I greatly prefer William Blake's "For everything that lives is holy" to Deuteronomy's Yahweh, obsessed with his own holiness, but neither Blake's fervor nor my wistfulness can affect human longings for transcendence. We seek secular transcendence in art, yet Shakespeare, supreme among artists, evades the holy, wisely aware of the limits of even his own reinvention of the human.

I distrusted, throughout this book, every account available to us of the historical Jesus, and I have been unable to locate much of an identity between the Jew from Nazareth and the theological God Jesus Christ. The human being Jesus and the all-too-human God Yahweh are more compatible (to me) than either is with Jesus the Christ and God the Father. I cannot regard that as a happy conclusion, and am all too aware of how unacceptable to believing Christians this must be. Yet I neither trust in the Covenant nor in Freud nor in Sam Harris's reductive opposition of "the future of reason" to religious terror. The need (or craving) for transcendence may well be a great unwisdom, but without it we tend to become mere engines of entropy. Yahweh, present *and* absent, has more to do with the end of trust than with the end of faith. Will he yet make a covenant with us that he both can and will keep?